Step-by-Step Guides

Word for Windows

Other titles in the Step-by-Step Series:

Lotus 1-2-3

D-Base III

WordPerfect

Microsoft Word

Microsoft Works

SuperCalc

WordStar

Paradox

Step-by-Step Guides

Word for Windows

Lisa Thomas MSc, MIPM, MITD
&
Richard Thomas MSc, BSc(Hons), Cert Ed

Stanley Thornes (Publishers) Ltd

First published in 1992 by:
Stanley Thornes (Publishers) Ltd
Old Station Drive
Leckhampton
CHELTENHAM GL53 0DN
England

A catalogue record for this book
is available from the British Library.

ISBN 0-7487-1514-2

Typeset by The New Leaf Book Company, Cheltenham, Glos.
Printed and bound in Great Britain at The Bath Press, Avon

CONTENTS

Using this Tutorial   1

The Keyboard   2

Getting Started   4

Lesson 1: Creating and Editing a Document   7

Lesson 2: Further Editing   16

Lesson 3: Printing   26

Lesson 4: Blocking Text   32

Lesson 5: Document Layout   41

Lesson 6: Formatting Documents   52

Lesson 7: Advanced Editing   59

Lesson 8: Merging Documents   67

Additional Exercises in Word for Windows   76

Alternative Methods   79

Further Word for Windows Facilities   80

Summary of Commands   81

Word for Windows Screen   82

Tool Bar   83

Ribbon   84

Getting out of Difficulties   85

USING THIS TUTORIAL

This learning pack is divided into a number of *lessons*. Each lesson covers a specific area and is further split into many graded *examples,* some of which build directly on previous examples. If possible, work through a whole lesson in a single session.

Each lesson ends with a short *test,* enabling you to check that you understand the contents of that lesson. If you are already familiar with some aspects of Word for Windows, you could use these tests as a method of revision without going through the complete lesson. Each test is followed by additional exercises to give you extra practice if required.

The lessons build on each other, with each incorporating skills from earlier lessons. However, every lesson is a complete unit, allowing you to pick out only those you require without going through the entire package. You should allow approximately one hour for each lesson. The test and further exercises will take extra time. The actual time will largely depend on your previous experience and keyboard skills.

Additional exercises are provided at the end of the lessons, covering the main aspects of the work outlined in the text. There are then some notes on further Word for Windows facilities not covered in the main text.

If you wish to use the program even more effectively, you should then look at the subsequent two chapters. The first lists alternative methods for carrying out procedures: these are keyboard short cuts which will help to increase your operating speed, while the second gives an explanation of further Word for Windows facilities

For those who have not previously used Windows there is a section describing the Word for Windows basic screen which will be particularly useful. This section is followed by a detailed description of the elements in the 'Toolbar' and 'Ribbon' areas contained in the basic screen.

Finally, for quick reference, a summary of commands is given at the back of the book, together with a section called 'Getting out of Difficulties' in case you have any problems while getting used to Word for Windows.

THE KEYBOARD

If you are not familiar with a computer keyboard, it is worth reading through this introduction before proceeding to the tutorials.

There are a few important keys you should know about:

THE ALT KEY

This key is labelled `Alt` This key can be used to activate the menu while you are in your document. This will be necessary if you are not using a mouse.

THE ARROW KEYS

These are labelled `←` `→` `↑` `↓`. On some keyboards they may be included on the extra numeric keypad to the right of the main keyboard. In this case, the **\<Num Lock\>** should be turned off.

These keys are used for moving the cursor around the screen: left, right, up or down; and can be used when selecting options on a menu.

THE BACKSPACE KEY

This is labelled `←` and is situated at the top right-hand corner of the letters keyboard. It can be used to delete characters already typed in. Press this once and you will delete the preceding character.

THE CAPS LOCK KEY

This is labelled `Caps Lock`. Its position varies from keyboard to keyboard. If you press this once, the Caps Lock light will come on and any letters you type will be produced in capitals. Pressing **\<Caps Lock\>** again will turn it off and any letters you type will be produced in lower-case letters.

THE CONTROL KEY

This is often labelled `Ctrl`. It can be used in conjunction with other keys to produce certain effects, such as moving the cursor quickly and improving text presentation.

THE ESCAPE KEY

This is usually labelled `Esc`. In Word for Windows, pressing the Escape key (**\<Esc\>**) will cancel what you are doing at that moment and take you back into your document.

THE RETURN KEY

This often looks like `↵` and is a large key situated to the right of the letter keys. It may be labelled **Enter** or **Return** instead of being marked with an arrow.

The Return or Enter key is used to enter information. It can be used wherever you are asked to press **\<Enter\>** in the tutorial.

THE SPACE BAR

This is the long key located at the bottom of the main keyboard. When you are asked to press <**Space**> you should press the space bar. This can be used to turn the options on or off in a selection screen if you are not using a mouse.

THE SHIFT KEY

This often looks like ⬆. There are two shift keys on your keyboard situated to the left and right of the letters.

The key is used for two reasons:

i) It produces capital letters.
    Hold <**Shift**> down and press a letter and you will obtain a capital letter.
ii) It produces alternative characters.
    Some keys have two characters printed on them. For example, near the top right-hand corner of the main keyboard you will see the key ± .
    If you press this, it produces =
    If you hold the <**Shift**> key down and also press this key, you get +

    Try this yourself with other keys. For example, type * or £ using the Shift key.

GETTING STARTED

WHAT IS WORD FOR WINDOWS?

Microsoft Word for Windows is a very powerful word processing package that can be used with a keyboard and/or a mouse.

A word processor allows you to create and edit documents easily and quickly. Using a word processor, you can edit text and produce printed documents of the highest quality.

In order to use the Word for Windows package Windows must already be set up on your computer. Windows provides an environment which is generally much easier to work in. Please ensure that Windows has been fully installed before proceeding with the Word package.

RUNNING WORD FOR WINDOWS

1 The system prompt is displayed on your screen (e.g. **C:>**)

Type **WIN** and press **<Return>** to start running Windows.

2 The `Word` icon will now be displayed on your screen. (If it is not, check that Word for Windows has been installed on your computer.)

Select the `Word` icon.

Either Use the mouse to double click on the `Word` icon.

or Use the arrow keys to move to the `Word` icon and then press **<Return>**

NOTES

An alternative method of loading Word for Windows direct from the system prompt is to type WIN WINWORD and press **<Return>**

3 The Word for Windows package has now been loaded and you are presented with a blank document as shown at the top of the next page.

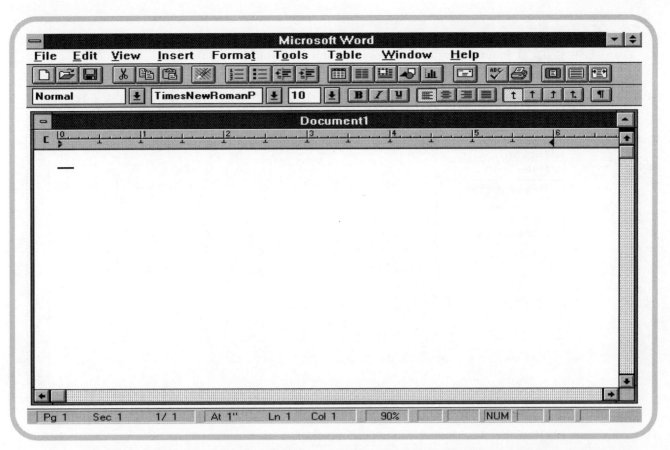

This screen contains a blank area for text editing in addition to the Menu, Ribbon, Toolbar and Ruler sections. Further details on the Ribbon and Toolbar are given at the end of this book.

ACTIVATING THE MENU

The menu shown near the top of the screen includes options such as **File** **Edit** **View** and **Insert** . This menu can be activated (and the options chosen) by using the mouse or the keyboard.

Either i) Use the mouse to point to the required option and click the Left Mouse Button

or i) Press the **<Alt>** key and then:

Either Move the highlight to the required option and press **<Return>**

or Type the underlined letter of the required option.

This process is demonstrated in the following section.

CHANGING THE SCREEN DISPLAY

When using Word for Windows you will need to select screen options. Try this now by choosing the **View** option to change the display of your screen.

1 Choose **View** either by:

Clicking on the **View** option, *or*

Pressing **<Alt>** then **V**

2 The options under **View** are displayed as shown at the top of the next page.

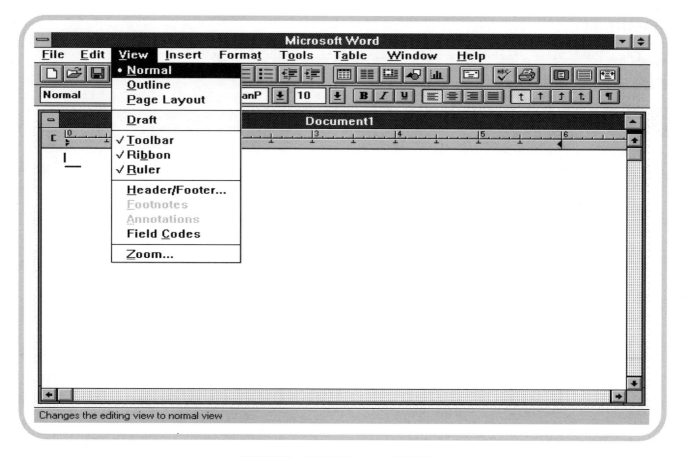

You see that the options **Toolbar** **Ribbon** and **Ruler** are displayed here.

To turn the Toolbar display on or off select the Toolbar option.

Either Click on **Toolbar**

or Type **T**

You now see that the Toolbar has been turned off and is no longer displayed. Compare your current screen with the screen illustrated in the previous section.

3 Similarly, you can use the **View** option to turn off the Ribbon and Ruler. Try this now.

4 Finally, use **View** to turn on all three options so that your screen is displayed as shown in the previous screen.

You have now started using the options in Word for Windows.

You are ready to start this tutorial. Turn to Lesson 1: Creating and Editing a Document.

Lesson 1:

CREATING AND EDITING A DOCUMENT

In this session we will look at creating a short document and basic editing facilities.

At the end of this lesson you will be able to:

- create a new document
- insert and delete text
- move the cursor
- save the document
- exit from Word for Windows.

Load Word for Windows. A blank page will be displayed on your screen.

EXAMPLE 1: CREATING A DOCUMENT

Create a document containing a short piece of text.

Use the following text for this example:

> A word processor allows us to create and edit documents quickly and easily. There are many word processing packages available. Word for Windows is one example of such a package.

Ensure that the Word for Windows package is loaded and a blank screen displayed.

METHOD

1 Type in the text given above. Use the **<Shift>** key to produce capital letters when required, and use the **<Backspace>** key to delete text when you make a mistake. (The **<Backspace>** key is found at the top right-hand corner of the main keyboard, and is often labelled ⬅)

Do not press the **<Return>** key at the end of each line. The word processor will automatically go to a new line when the first line is filled up.

The screen will now display the text as shown at the top of the next page.

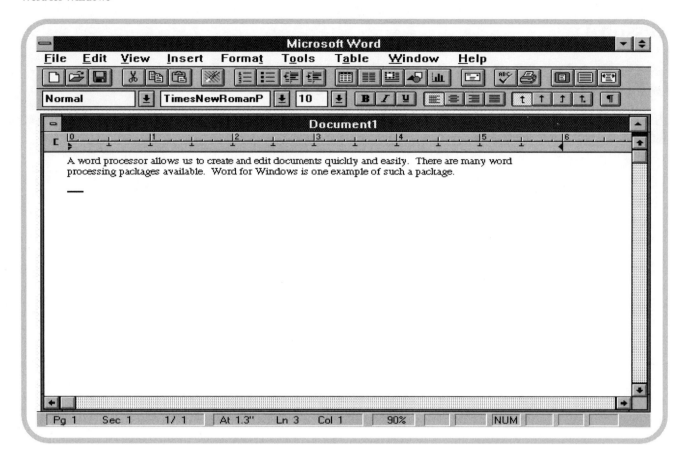

EXAMPLE 2: INSERTING TEXT

Insert the word 'very' before 'quickly' in the first line on the document you have created.

You can move the cursor to any position in your document using the mouse.

Simply move the pointer to the position required and click the left mouse button.

Alternatively, you can move the cursor around the screen using the arrow keys.

The four keys ← → ↑ ↓ allow you to move left, right, up and down in your document.

METHOD

1 Use the mouse to move the cursor position to the 'q' of 'quickly' in the first sentence. (Alternatively use the arrow keys.)

2 Now type **very** and press **<Space>**

You will see that this word and the extra space is now inserted in the text and the document has been re-arranged to accommodate the extra word.

EXAMPLE 3: DELETING TEXT

Delete the words 'and easily' from the document.

METHOD

1 Use the mouse or arrow keys to move the cursor to the 'a' at the start of 'and easily'.

2 Now press the **<Delete>** key. (This is marked **Del** on some keyboards, and is found near the arrow keys.)

Each time you press the **<Delete>** key, you will remove one character. The remaining text is moved in to fill the gap.

3 Keep pressing the **<Delete>** key until the required words ('and easily') have been removed.

NOTES

There are two basic ways of deleting text. You can either use the **<Delete>** key to delete characters at the cursor, or the **<Backspace>** key to delete characters to the left of the cursor.

EXAMPLE 4: INSERTING HEADINGS

Insert the title 'WORD PROCESSING' at the top of the document.

METHOD

1 Move the cursor to the beginning of the first line in your text.

2 Type **WORD PROCESSING**

3 Press **<Return>**

You will see that by pressing **<Return>** all the text starting at the cursor has moved down to a new line.

4 Press **<Return>** again.

You now have a tidy document where the title is separated from the text by a blank line.

5 Press **<Return>** a few more times. You will see that this is a way of moving all the text down. Now press **<Backspace>** a few times to delete these extra returns: the text will move back up.

The document will now be displayed as shown below:

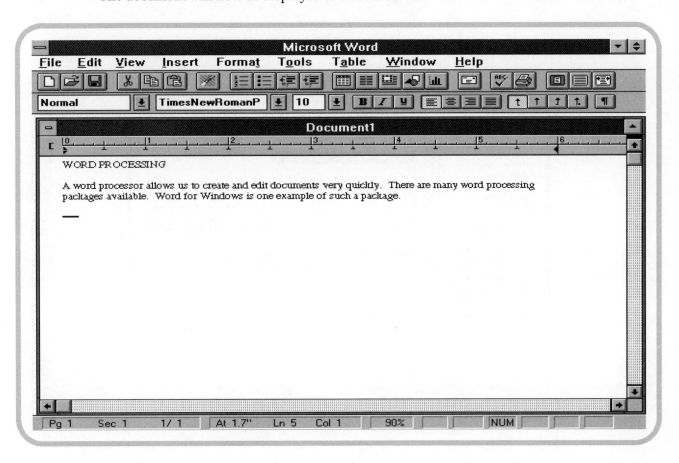

EXAMPLE 5: SAVING DOCUMENTS

Save the document you have just created as a file called WORD1

METHOD

1 There are a number of ways you can save a document. Try experimenting with each of these routines:

 i)   Use the mouse to click on the 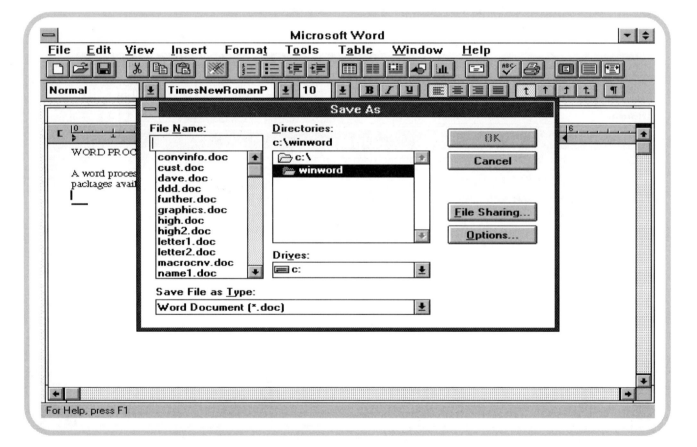 icon near the top of the screen or

 ii) Use the mouse to click on the **File** option at the top of the screen.

      Click on **Save** or

 iii) Press **<Alt>** and **F** to select the File menu.

      Now choose the **Save** option (either by moving the highlight down to **Save** and pressing **<Return>** or by typing **S**).

2 The following screen is displayed:

3 This screen shows which directory will be used to save this file e.g. **C:\WINWORD**. (You may have a different directory specified depending on how your package has been set up. Do not change it for this example.)

4 Type the name of the file you wish to save.

 Type **WORD1** and press **<Return>**

5 At this stage you may be required to enter some other details (e.g. title, subject, etc.).

 Press **<Return>** to proceed without entering any details.

The document has now been saved, and you are back in the text.

The top line of the screen now displays the name of this document: **WORD1.DOC.** (All documents saved in Word have a filename followed by **.DOC** unless when saving the file you have specified something different.)

EXAMPLE 6: EXITING FROM WORD

Exit from the package to finish.

METHOD

1 Select the **File** option.

(Either by using the mouse to click on **File** or pressing **<Alt>** and **F**)

2 Now choose **Exit** (either by clicking on **Exit** or typing **E**).

If you have made changes to the text since saving, a message will appear at the bottom of the screen asking you whether you wish to save the changes to this document. You can then choose **Yes** (to save) or **No** (to quit without saving) or **Cancel** (to return to the document).

Select **Yes** or **No**

3 You are now out of the Word for Windows package.

TEST

1 Load the Word for Windows package.

2 Create a document with the following text:

Word processing involves using a computer to create letters, memos, charts or any other document that you can create on a typewriter.

You first write or create the documents and save them on a disk. Whatever you type is displayed on the screen. With a word processor, you can easily add to, change, correct or erase single letters, words, paragraphs or entire documents.The documents can then be printed as many times as you require.

3 Insert the title 'WHAT IS WORD PROCESSING?' at the top of this document.

4 Delete the sentence 'Whatever you type is displayed on the screen.'

5 Insert a new paragraph at the bottom of the document:

Completed documents are stored electronically on a diskette or hard disk, and can be changed, edited or updated whenever you wish.

6 Save this document as WORD2 and exit from Word.

FURTHER EXERCISES

1 i) Create a document containing the following text:

The WORD FOR WINDOWS package consists of a range of menus and icons in order to assist in the use of all facilities. The icons and menu are displayed at the top of the screen and the menu can be activated any time by pressing the Alt key or using the mouse.

The File menu can be used in order to save documents you have created, and to retrieve old files.

ii) In the first sentence, delete 'consists of' and replace with 'provides'.

iii) Insert the title 'USE OF THE MENU' at the top of this document. Put blank lines after the title and between the two paragraphs.

iv) Save the document as MENUBAR.

2 i) Create a document containing the letter given below:

Dear Madam

Thank you for your letter dated 29 September requesting a copy of the WORD FOR WINDOWS package. Details on prices and how to order are enclosed with this letter.

Yours sincerely

Violet Gregory

ii) Save this document as ORDER1.

iii) Insert a date and your address at the top of the letter.

iv) Replace 'sincerely' with 'faithfully'.

v) Re-save this letter as ORDER1.

You are now ready to go on to Lesson 2: Further Editing.

Lesson 2:

FURTHER EDITING

In this session we will look at additional editing facilities within Word for Windows.

At the end of this lesson you will be able to:

- retrieve documents
- move the cursor quickly
- use tabs
- erase the screen
- create tables
- centre text.

Load Word for Windows. A blank page will be displayed on your screen.

EXAMPLE 1: RETRIEVING A DOCUMENT

Retrieve a document called WORD2 which you have already saved on disk. (WORD2 was created in the test at the end of Lesson 1. If you have not completed this, you can use the document WORD1 for this lesson.)

METHOD

1   You can retrieve (or open) a file in a number of ways.

   Either   i)   Using the mouse click on the icon

   or   ii)   Using the mouse click on the   **File**   option and then click on   **Open**

   or   iii)   Press **<Alt>** and **F**

            Now choose the   **Open**   option.

2   The screen is now displayed as shown at the top of the next page.

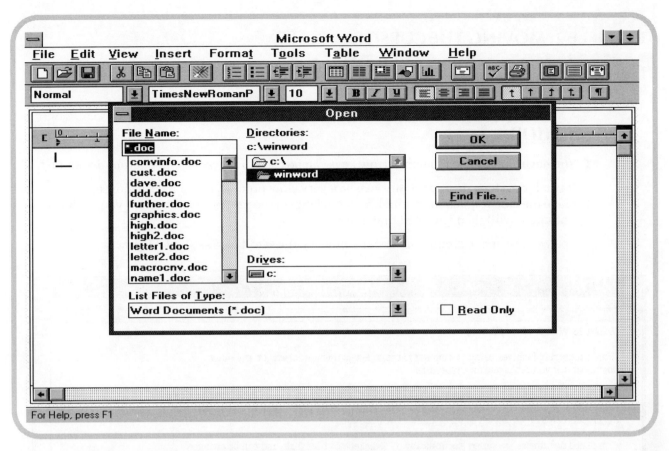

3 Type in the required filename, e.g. type **WORD2** and press **<Return>**

This document is now displayed on your screen as shown below:

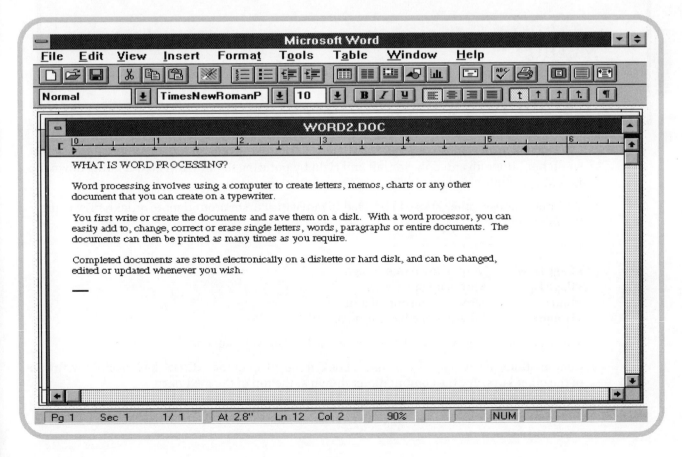

Notice that the document name (e.g. WORD2.DOC) appears at the top of the screen.

EXAMPLE 2: MOVING THE CURSOR

Learn how to move the cursor around your document quickly.

METHOD

1 You have already seen that the arrow keys can be used to move the cursor around your text.

If you have a long document, this can be a very slow process. If you have a mouse, you can move the cursor much more quickly by clicking on the part of the document you wish to edit. The cursor will then appear at that point.

You can also move around the document using the scroll bars as shown below:

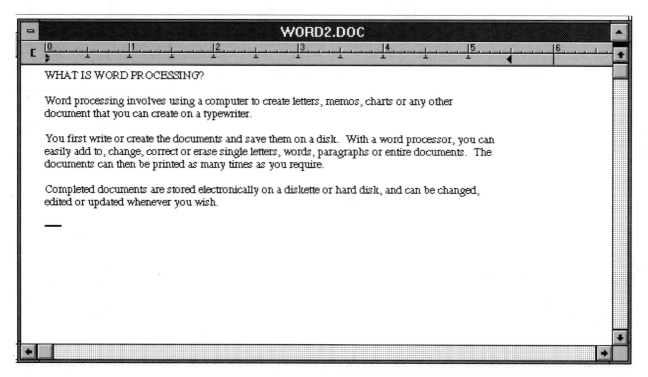

Click on the arrows in these scroll bars to move around the document. Alternatively, drag the scroll box either up and down or left and right by pointing to the scroll box, holding down the Left Mouse Button and moving the pointer to a new position.

Without a mouse, other keys can be used to move the cursor around more quickly. Try using the following keys:

Key	Effect
<Page Down>	Moves down one screen
<Page Up>	Moves up one screen
<End>	Moves to the end of a line
<Home>	Moves to the beginning of a line

These keys are usually located near the arrow keys on your keyboard.

2 Combinations of keys can also be used. Look at the effect of the **<Ctrl>** key together with one of the other keys. Try the combinations shown at the top of the next page.

Key	*Effect*
<Ctrl> →	Moves one word to the right
<Ctrl> ←	Moves one word to the left
<Ctrl> ↑	Moves to the previous paragraph
<Ctrl> ↓	Moves to the next paragraph
<Ctrl> <Home>	Moves to the beginning of the document
<Ctrl> <End>	Moves to the end of the document

You do not need to remember these, but they may be useful later when you are producing longer documents.

EXAMPLE 3: USING TABS

Use the **<Tab>** key to indent the start of each paragraph

METHOD

1 Move the cursor to the beginning of the first paragraph.

2 Press the **<Tab>** key.

(It is situated on the top left-hand side of the keyboard next to the letter 'Q'.)

You will see that the text on this line has moved to the right by a number of spaces.

3 Move the cursor to the beginning of the next paragraph and press the **<Tab>** key.

4 Continue to do this for all the paragraphs in this document. The document will be displayed as shown below:

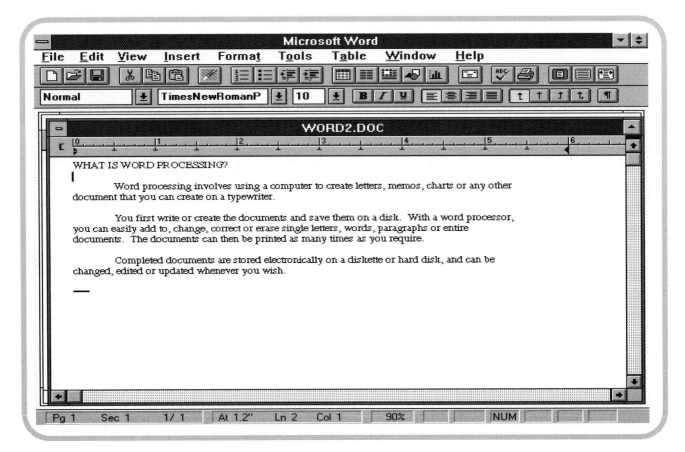

5 If you prefer the original display, go back and delete the tabs by moving the cursor to the first letter in a paragraph and pressing the **<Backspace>** key.

EXAMPLE 4: RE-SAVING AND ERASING

Save the amended document and erase from the screen.

METHOD

1 Firstly, save this document.

    Either   i)   Click on the   🖫   icon

    or   ii)   Click on   **File**   and   **Save**

    or   iii)   Press   **\<Alt\>**   and   **F**   and choose   **Save**

The file has automatically been saved under the same name (e.g. WORD2).

NOTES

If you want to re-save a document using a different filename you must select   **File**   and choose   **Save As**   You will now be able to type in a new file name.

2 To erase the screen we must close the document currently displayed.

Select   **File**   (either click on   **File**   or press   **\<Alt\>**   and **F**).

Select   **Close**   (either click on   **Close**   or type   **C**).

If you have made any changes to the document since saving you will be asked whether you wish to save the changes.

Select   **Yes**   or   **No**   here.

3 The screen will now be cleared.

EXAMPLE 5: CREATING TABLES

Create a new document containing the quarterly sales figures for a company over a four–year period.

Use the following information in your table.

QUARTERLY SALES 1992–1995

	1992	1993	1994	1995
1st Quarter	300	625	720	870
2nd Quarter	450	850	825	885
3rd Quarter	500	700	910	910
4th Quarter	520	600	890	960

METHOD

1 Select **File**

Choose **New**

Now click on **OK** or press **<Return>**

A blank document should now be displayed.

2 Type **QUARTERLY SALES 1992–1995**

Press **<Return>** twice.

3 Press **<Tab>** three times.

Type **1992**

4 Similarly, press **<Tab>** twice and type **1993**

Press **<Tab>** twice and type **1994**

Press **<Tab>** twice and type **1995**

Press **<Return>** twice.

5 Now type **1st Quarter**

Now enter **<Tab> <Tab> 300 <Tab> <Tab> 625 <Tab> <Tab> 720 <Tab> <Tab> 870**

Press **<Return>**

NOTES

The number of tabs you require to create this document will depend on where the tab settings are placed. In Lesson 5: Document Layout, you will be shown how to change the tab settings in your document. At this stage simply use the current tab settings.

6 Similarly, enter the other values, using the **<Tab>** key as much as possible.

The document you have created will look like the one displayed at the top of the next page.

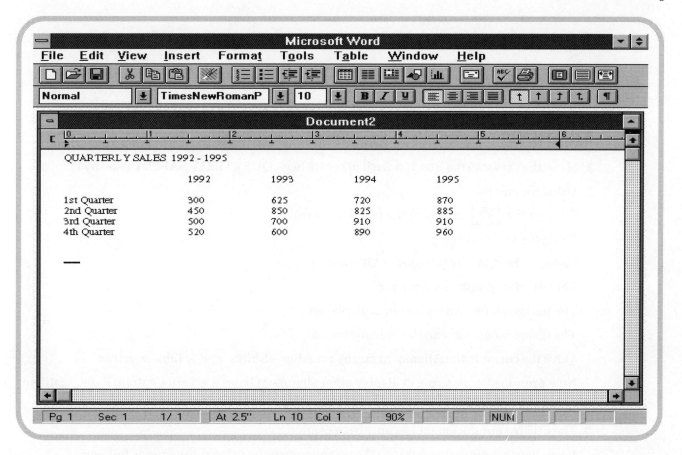

EXAMPLE 6: CENTERING TEXT

Centre the heading in your document.

METHOD

1 Move the cursor to the line you wish to centre (e.g. **QUARTERLY SALES 1992–1995**)

2 *Using the mouse:*

Click on the ☰ icon near the top of the screen.

Using the keyboard:

Choose **Format** by pressing **<Alt>** and **T**

Choose **Paragraph** by typing **P**

The paragraph formatting screen is displayed.

The cursor is currently on the Indentation box.

Move the cursor to the Alignment box by pressing **<Shift>** and **<Tab>** together.

Now press the Down arrow to display other alignment types e.g. Left, Centred, Right, Justified.

Select the **Centred** option and press **<Return>**

3 The title in your document has now been centred.

If you have a mouse, try to change the text alignment by using the menus as follows:

Click on **Format**

Click on **Paragraph**

Now click on the Alignment box and choose a different alignment, e.g. Left or Right.

Now click on **OK**

4 Finally, save this document with the title centred, as a file called SALES

NOTES

If required, you can turn the centering off by using either the ☰ icon or choosing the **Format** and **Paragraph** options and selecting an alternative alignment (e.g. Left).

TEST

1 Erase the screen (ensure that you have already saved the previous document).

2 Using the TAB key when required, create a new document containing the following details:

Employee	Grade	Salary
M GREGORY	A12	£14,500
R THOMAS	B13	£18,175
M MANSFIELD	A07	£14,700
D MATTHEWS	B17	£12,500
S MCCANN	C02	£9,200
H WRIGHT	A06	£16,750
S SINGH	A04	£21,200
S SLATER	B14	£12,140
M BANBURY	A07	£19,150
T BASI	C11	£16,250
L KNOTT	B19	£13,120

3 Insert a title for this table: EMPLOYEE SUMMARY

4 Centre the title.

5 Save this document as EMPLOYEE and erase the screen.

FURTHER EXERCISES

1 i) Create a table of names and addresses as shown below:

J Brand	R Rubens
2 New Hill	34 The Walkway
Glasgow	Coventry
R Sangha	G Gregory
269 High Street	72 Wilton Avenue
Plymouth	Ramsgate
A Forsyth	B Jung
177 Jarvis Close	85 The Avenue
Newquay	Londonderry

   ii)   Insert the title 'MAILING LIST' and centre this line.
   iii) Change the address of A Forsyth to '243 Winter Close, Barnstable'.
   iv) Save this file as MAILING and close the document.

2 i)   Retrieve a document called EMPLOYEE (this was created in the test section above)
   ii)   Insert a company name at the top of this document: 'THE ABS PROVINCIAL COMPANY'. Centre this on the line.
   iii) Delete two employees – S MCCANN and T BASI – from the list.
   iv) Insert a new employee at the top of the list:

G BIGGS	B12	£14,300

   v)   Re-save this document as EMP2

You are now ready to go on to Lesson 3: Printing.

Lesson 3:

PRINTING

In this session you will look at printing documents that have been created.

At the end of this lesson you will be able to:

- print a document
- preview a document
- obtain multiple copies
- obtain a list of files.

Load Word for Windows. A blank page will be displayed on your screen.

EXAMPLE 1: PRINTING A DOCUMENT

Open a file called WORD2 and print it out. (WORD2 was created in the test section at the end of Lesson 1 and modified in Lesson 2. Any other document can be used in this example if required.)

METHOD

1 Select `File` and `Open`

   Now choose the appropriate document.

   Either i) type **WORD2** and press **<Return>**

   or   ii) click on the `WORD2. DOC` in the list of files and click on `OK`

2 The document can be printed out in a number of ways:

   Either i) click on the icon

   or   ii) select `File` and `Print`

   The document will now be displayed on your screen as shown at the top of the next page.

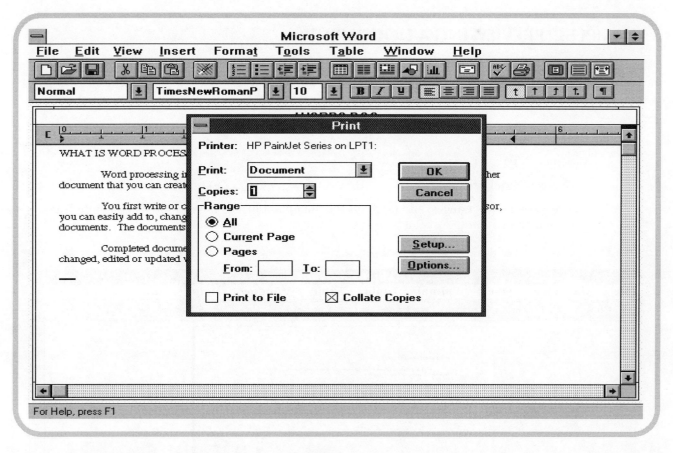

Now press **<Return>** or click on OK

3 A print-out of your document will now be produced. If you have any problems with obtaining a print-out, check that your printer is connected and has been set up correctly.

EXAMPLE 2: PREVIEWING A DOCUMENT

Using the same file that you now have on the screen (WORD2), view the document before printing.

METHOD

1 Select **File**

2 Choose **Print Preview**

The screen now changes, and displays the document just as it will look when printed, as shown below:

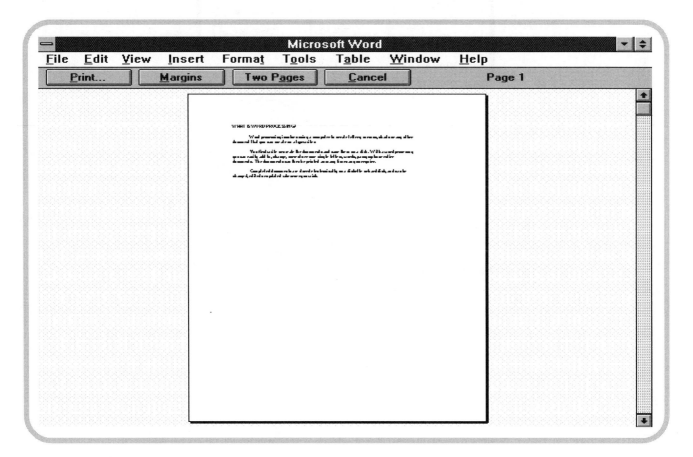

3 You can now use the **<Page Up>** and **<Page Down>** keys to look at other pages in a long document.

You can choose **Print** to print out this document or **Cancel** to return to the text.

EXAMPLE 3: PRINTING MULTIPLE COPIES

Print out two copies of the document you have on screen.

METHOD

1 A document (e.g. WORD2) should be displayed on your screen.

Select **File**

Choose **Print**

2 A print window is now displayed as shown below:

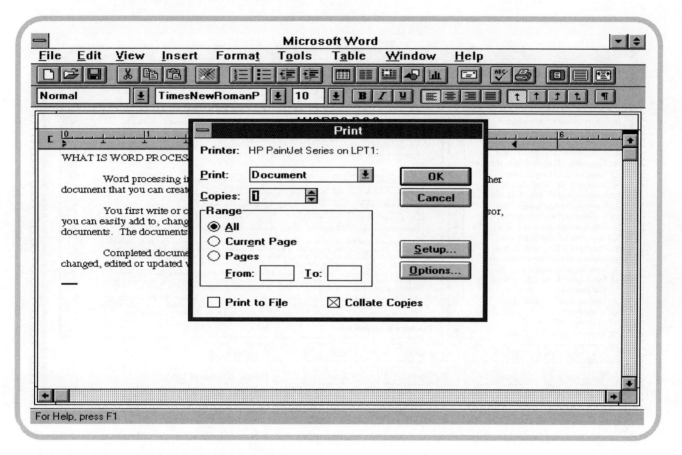

The cursor is in the Copies box.

Choose the number of copies required.

Either i) Type **2** and press **<Return>**

or   ii) Click on the Up arrow in this box to change the number of copies and then click on **OK**

3 Two copies of this document will now be printed.

The document is displayed on your screen again.

EXAMPLE 4: FINDING FILES

Review a list of documents before printing.

METHOD

This procedure is useful when you cannot remember the name or contents of a document.

1 Select **File**

Now choose **Find File**

The following screen is displayed:

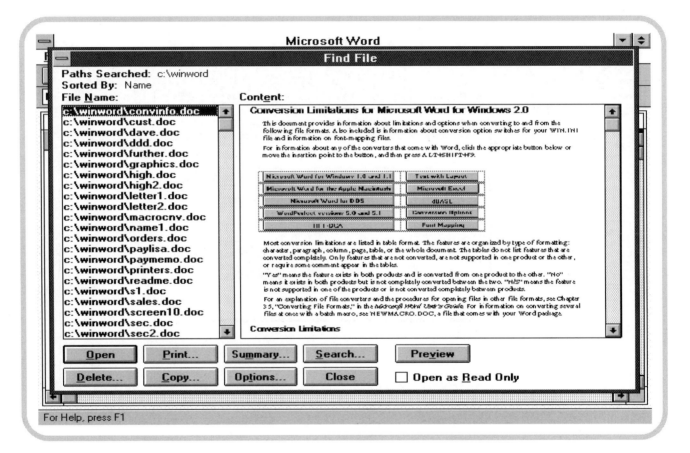

2 The screen now shows a list of files in the current directory. The first filename is highlighted. The right side of the screen shows the contents of the first page of this file.

NOTES

If you have problems obtaining a list here you may be looking in the wrong Directory. If so, you can choose **Search** to change the Directory. Alternatively choose **Close** to exit from this screen.

Now select **File** and then choose **Open** Now change to the required Directory.

Click on **OK**

Now select **Find File**

3 Move the highlight down to the required file, e.g. WORD2. Notice that the contents of this document are shown on the right of the screen.

4 Other options are available such as **Print** (to print out the highlighted file) or **Delete**

5 Select **Close** to exit from this screen.

TEST

1 Close the current file.

2 Obtain a list of files on your current directory. Now open a selected file from this list, e.g. SALES.

3 Use the Print options to preview this document.

4 Obtain two copies of this document.

5 Close the document.

FURTHER EXERCISES

1 i) Create a new document containing the following text:

Dear Ms Gomez

Many thanks for your letter dated 27 September. I am pleased to inform you that we are currently running a number of word processing training courses.

If you require any further details, please contact me at the above address.

Yours sincerely

A Khan
Training and Development Manager

ii) Edit this letter to include your own address and today's date.

iii) View this document to see how it will be printed.

iv) Insert a second paragraph stating:

One day WORD FOR WINDOWS courses are being held on the following dates:

18 February
12 June
29 September

Each course runs from 9.30 a.m. to 4.30 p.m. and costs £200 per delegate.

v) Print out two copies of this letter.

2 i) Retrieve the MENUBAR document. (This was created in the Further Exercises section at the end of Lesson 1. Any document can be used for this exercise.)

ii) View this document to see how it will look when printed.

iii) Print out a copy of this document.

iv) Close the file.

You are now ready to go on to Lesson 4: Moving Text.

Lesson 4:

BLOCKING TEXT

In this session we will deal with editing blocks of text within a document.

At the end of this lesson you will be able to:

- select a block of text
- move a block of text to a new position
- paste a block of text
- copy a block of text
- delete a block of text
- copy text to a new file.

Load Word for Windows. A blank page will be displayed on your screen.

EXAMPLE 1: CREATING A LETTER

Create a document containing a letter; and save the document as LETTER1.

Use the following text for your letter:

32 Bourne Avenue
Easthampton
PX21 4KB

2 June 1994

Dear Mr Lewis

Thank you for your letter dated 25 May. We have an extensive range of the items you require and I enclose a brochure together with the latest price list. Your letter contained a detailed list of requirements. The following items are always in stock:

    Print Ribbons
    Diskettes
    Stationery

If you require any further details, please do not hesitate to contact me.

Yours sincerely

Hannah Gregory
Marketing Manager

METHOD

1 Select **File** and **Open** to create a new document.

Type in the text using tabs where appropriate.

2 Now save this document.

Either i) Click on the 💾 icon.

or ii) Choose **File** and **Save**

3 The **Save As** window is displayed.

Type in the name of the new document

e.g. **LETTER1**

Press **<Return>** or click on **OK**

4 The **Summary Information** window is now displayed.

Type in some details here:

e.g. **Title:**   **Letter to Mr Lewis**

(Do *not* press **<Return>** . Use the **<Tab>** key or the mouse to move to the next field.)

        Subject: **Sales**

When you have finished press **<Return>** or click on **OK**

The file has now been saved including any summary information you have added.

EXAMPLE 2: SELECTING TEXT

Experiment with selecting blocks of text in your document.

You have to select text before you can use a number of Word for Windows facilities such as moving, deleting and copying blocks of text.

Text can be selected by using the mouse or the keyboard as shown in the method given below.

METHOD

1 *Using the mouse*:

Move the mouse pointer to the beginning of the text you wish to select.

Click on the left button and keep the button pressed down while you drag the cursor to the end of the text to be selected.

The text is now highlighted. (Clicking the button anywhere else in the document will remove this highlighting.)

2 *Using the keyboard:*

Move the cursor to the beginning of the text you wish to select by using the arrow keys.

Hold down the **<Shift>** key while using the arrow keys to move the cursor to the end of the text to be selected.

The text is now highlighted.

3 Using the methods given above select the first paragraph in the document you have on screen.

4 Now change the selection by highlighting a different block of text.

You will need to use these methods for selecting text in the following examples in this lesson.

EXAMPLE 3: MOVING TEXT

Edit the letter created in Example 1 (LETTER1) by moving the sentence 'Your letter contained...' to the position immediately after the first sentence ('Thank you for...').

METHOD

1 Place the cursor at the beginning of the text to be moved (i.e. 'Your letter...').

2 Select the required sentence using one of the methods described in Example 2.

   The text should now be highlighted

3 We wish to delete this text from the current position and insert it into a new position.

   Choose **Edit**

   Now select **Cut**

   (Alternatively, click on the ✂ icon.)

   The block of text has now been deleted from your document and saved in a temporary location.

4 Move the cursor to the required new position: i.e. at the beginning of the sentence 'We have an extensive...'

5 Choose **Edit**

   Now select **Paste**

   (Alternatively, click on the 📋 icon)

   The block of text will now be inserted into your document.

   The screen display will look like the one given below:

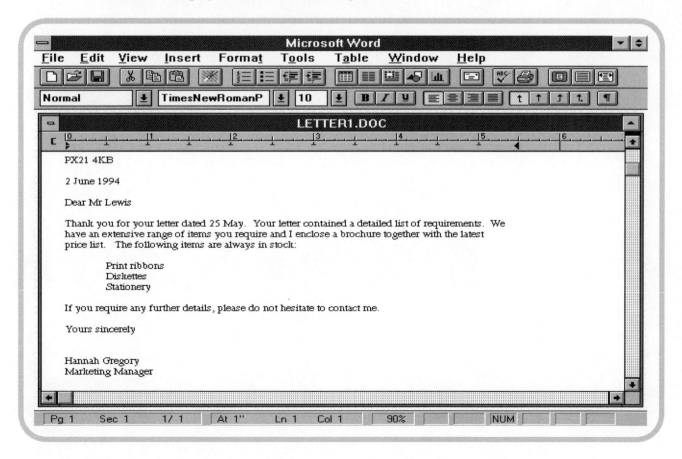

6 Save the document:

Select **File** and **Save**

(or click on the icon)

The amended letter has now ben re-saved as LETTER1

EXAMPLE 4: PASTING TEXT

Insert the same block of text into a new position in the document.

The block of text you have already moved can be pasted as many times as you like into your document.

METHOD

1 Move the cursor to the new position in which you wish to insert the text.

2 Choose **Edit** and **Paste** (or click on the ⊡ icon).

You have now inserted (or pasted) the same block of text into the document.

Delete this sentence before proceeding to the next example. Do this by highlighting the text and using **Edit** and **Cut**

EXAMPLE 5: COPYING TEXT

Copy one sentence in your document to a new position.

METHOD

1 Select the first sentence in the letter, so that the text is highlighted.

2 Choose **Edit** and **Copy**

(Alternatively, click on the [icon] icon.)

3 Move the cursor to a new position in your document, e.g. at the end of the paragraph.

4 Choose **Edit** and **Paste**

(Alternatively click on the [icon] icon.)

The selected text has now been copied to a new position.

You may wish to delete this sentence before continuing.

You can do this by choosing **Edit** and **Undo** (or clicking on the [icon] icon).

EXAMPLE 6: COPYING TEXT TO A NEW DOCUMENT

Insert the address in this letter (LETTER1) to a new document called LETTER2.

We can copy a block of text from an existing document into a new file.

METHOD

1 Select the address in the letter (LETTER1). The full address should be highlighted.

2 Choose **Edit** and **Copy**
(or click on the [icon] icon)

3 Now create a new file:

Either i) Choose **File** and **New**

Press **<Return>** or click on **OK**

or ii) Click on the [icon] icon

4 A new file has now been set up.

Now insert the text you have previously highlighted:

Either i) Choose **Edit** and **Paste**

or ii) Click on the [icon] icon

The address has now been inserted in this new document.

A new letter could now be produced including this address.

5 Now save this new letter:

Choose **File** and **Save**

Type **LETTER2 <Return>**

Enter summary details if required.

Press **<Return>** or click on **OK** to save.

6 Choose **File** and **Close** to close this document.

You will now see that the LETTER1 document is displayed.

Close this document in the same way (select **Yes** to save any changes if requested).

TEST

1 Create a new document called SEC and type in the following text:

RECRUITING A SECRETARY

The task of recruiting a secretary has changed considerably over the last ten years. In the past, the main selection criteria were typing and shorthand speeds. Some consideration may have been given to previous experience, and of course qualifications were, and still are, an important indication of ability.

Today the selection process is far more complex, the job criteria far wider. As well as verbal, numerical, typing and shorthand ability, we look for an interest and aptitude in the technical aspects of the job e.g. the use of various computer packages, fax machines, and electronic communication systems. Other important qualities include an ability to manage and organise, interpersonal skills and forward planning skills.

The role of the Secretary is key to the success of a department and even an organisation. It is easy to understand then, why employers are spending considerable time and money making sure they make the right decision.

2 Move the sentence in the final paragraph: 'it is easy to understand...' to a new position before the second paragraph.

3 Copy the sentence in the first paragraph: 'In the past...' to the beginning of the same paragraph. This sentence should now appear twice, so delete the second one.

4 Copy the title and first paragraph into a new document called SEC2.

5 Save this document as SEC and close the file.

FURTHER EXERCISES

1 i)   Create a new document containing the following list of employees.

Name	Salary
J Matthews	£22,000
A Ali	£20,000
S Rodaway	£17,650
M Thomas	£21,000
B Morris	£29,500
T Richard	£18,250
H Wright	£18,250
S Aqbal	£24,540
P Zanod	£15,720

ii)   Move the lines of text around so that the employees are listed in alphabetical order.

iii)   Delete the block containing the employees Richard and Rodaway.

iv)   Print out this document.

v)   Save the document as EMPLIST.

2 i)   Create a new document containing the following memo:

To: Head of Finance   From: Head of Personnel

The following staff will commence employment with us at the beginning of next month.

Would you please include them on the payroll, together with the appropriate pay scale. Further details on Grade and National Insurance are included in a separate document.

ii)   Copy the list of employees (EMPLIST) created in Question 1 (above) into the space between the first and second paragraphs.

iii)   Put the date and your name on this document and save it as EMPMEMO.

You are now ready to go on to Lesson 5: Document Layout.

Lesson 5:

DOCUMENT LAYOUT

In this session we will look at improving document layout and the display of text.

At the end of this lesson you will be able to:

- change margins
- set new tab positions
- underline and embolden text
- set page breaks
- indent paragraphs.

Load Word for Windows. A blank page will be displayed on your screen.

EXAMPLE 1: CHANGING MARGINS

Retrieve the document WORD2 and change the left and right margins.

METHOD

1 Retrieve the document:

Choose **File** and **Open**

Type **WORD2** or select it from the list using the mouse.

Press **<Return>** or click on **OK**

The document will now be displayed on your screen.

Margins can be changed in a number of ways. In this example we will look at two methods.

2 Select **Format** and **Page Setup**

The following screen is now displayed as shown at the top of the next page.

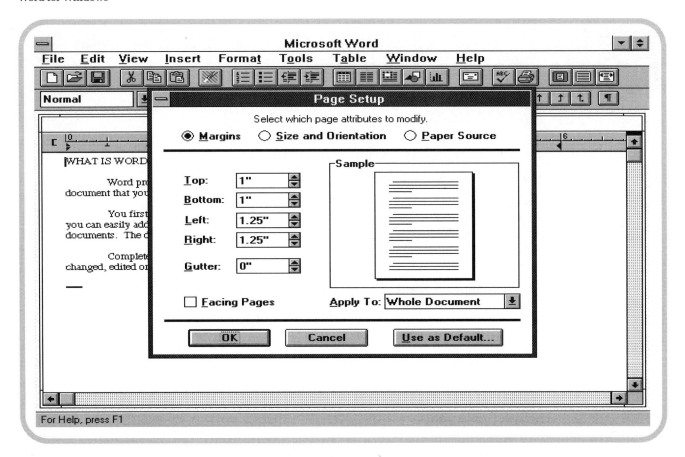

3 The margins are displayed in inches.

Move to the Left margin box using the mouse or **<Tab>** key.

Type **2** and press **<Return>** or click on **OK**

(You may need to delete other numbers already in this box.)

You will see that the document has been reformatted as a result of the changed left margin.

4 Similarly, change the right margin:

Select **Format** and **Page Setup**

Move to the Right margin box.

Type **3**

Press **<Return>** or click on **OK**

You will see that the layout of the document has changed.

Select **File** and **Print Preview** to see exactly how this document will look when printed.

5 An alternative method of changing margins is shown below:

Select **File** and **Print Preview**

Now select **Margins**

The following screen is displayed as shown at the top of the next page.

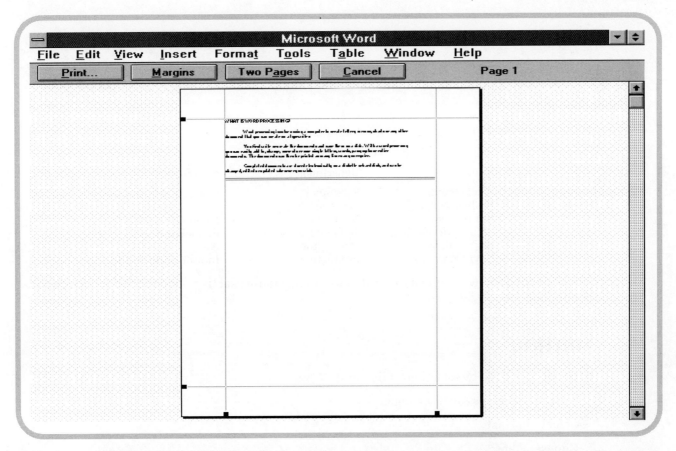

The margins are now displayed on the previewed document. Each margin has a small square (called a margin handle) located at the bottom or the side.

6 Now move a margin.

Either i) Use the mouse to point to a margin handle, then click and drag it to a new position.

or ii) Use the **<Tab>** key to move the cursor to the required margin handle. Use the arrow keys to move it to a new position and press **<Return>**

Then click on the mouse outside the page to show the reformatted document.

7 Now select **Cancel** to return to the document. Experiment with different margin widths and print out the resulting document. Do *not* save any of these changes.

Close this file before proceeding to the next example.

EXAMPLE 2: SETTING DEFAULT TAB STOPS

Set three tab stops in a new document and enter a table.

Use the following information in your document:

WORD COURSE DELEGATE LIST

Name	Department	Experience
Alicia Franklin	Personnel	None
Graham Nobes	Engineering	None
Julia Crouch	Marketing	Basic WP
Wendy McCleish	Technical Services	Some Word
Brian Batchelor	Production	None
David Warner	Production	Intermediate Word

When creating a new document it is often useful to choose exactly where you want the tabs to be positioned.

METHOD

1 Create a new file by selecting **File** and **New**

Now the tab stops can be changed:

Select **Format**

Choose **Tabs**

The following screen is displayed:

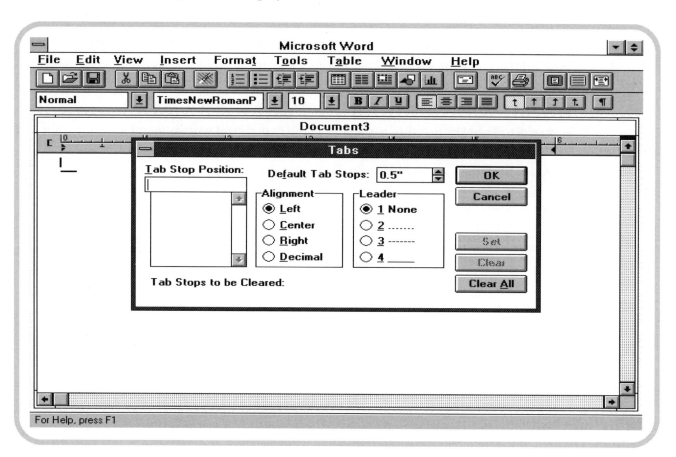

2 Now select **Clear All** to clear any previous tab settings.

At the Tab Stop Position type **0.5**

Now choose `Set`

Similarly, type **2.5** in the Tab Stop Position and choose `Set`

Finally type **4.5** in the Tab Stop Position and choose `Set`

(This has set the first Tab Stop at 0.5" and subsequent Tab Stops at 2.5" and 4.5".)

Press **<Return>** or click `OK`

3 Now use these tabs to insert the given text in the required columns.

Save this document as STAFF.

EXAMPLE 3: CHANGING TAB SETTINGS USING THE RULER

Use the ruler to change tab settings.

METHOD

1 The Ruler should be displayed just above your document.

(If not, select **View** and **Ruler** to turn on the display.)

2 Move the cursor to the bottom of the document. The four tab icons 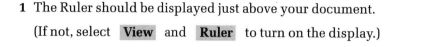 displayed near the top of the screen allow you to choose Left, Centre, Right and Decimal tabs.

Click on the required tab icon, e.g. [t] (Left Tab).

Now point to the position on the ruler where you want to insert a tab and click on the mouse. For example, try to set a tab at 2" by clicking just below the ruler line.

3 To remove a tab, click on the tab position and drag down and away from the ruler. For example, try to remove the tab setting at 2.5".

4 You can move existing tab settings by clicking and dragging left or right to a new position on the ruler.

For example, try to move the tab setting from 4.5" back to 4".

5 Now type in three more names at the bottom of this document using the tabs to check that these new tab settings are in operation.

Close this document without saving these changes.

EXAMPLE 4: HIGHLIGHTING NEW TEXT

Use underlining and emboldening to create a document.

Use the following text in your document.

<u>CHAPTER 1</u>

We can improve the image of our documents by utilising the underline and embolding facilities. We can highlight headings, new sections or specific words.

SECTION 1

In this particular document we can see that the Chapter Heading is underlined and the Section Heading is in bold type. Generally in the **Word for Windows** package any highlighting you use will automatically be displayed on the screen.

METHOD

1 Close the previous document and create a new file.

NOTES

When highlighting text you can use the mouse or the keyboard as follows:

	Mouse	Keyboard
on/off bold text	click on **B**	press **<Ctrl>** and **B**
on/off underlining	click on **U**	press **<Ctrl>** and **U**
on/off italics	click on *I*	press **<Ctrl>** and **I**
plain text		press **<Ctrl>** and **<Space>**

2 Now create the document as shown.

Turn Underline on (click on **U** or press **<Ctrl>** and **U**)

Type CHAPTER 1

Now centre this text.

Either i) Click on the ≡ (centre) icon.

or   ii) Choose **Format** and **Paragraph.** and select **Centered alignment**

3 Press **<Return>** to move to the next line.

Turn Underline off (click on the **U** icon or press **<Ctrl>** and **U**).

Turn Centering off:

Either i) Click on the ≡ (left align) icon

or   ii) Choose **Format** and **Paragraph.** and select **Left alignment**

4 Type in the first paragraph of text: 'We can improve the image of...'

5 Now turn the Bold on (click on the **B** icon or press **<Ctrl>** and **B**).

Type in **SECTION 1**

Turn the Bold off.

6 Type in the remaining text ensuring that the appropriate text is highlighted.

7 Save this document as HIGH and close the file.

EXAMPLE 5: HIGHLIGHTING EXISTING TEXT

Use Underlining and Bold to improve the display of the table given in the STAFF document.

METHOD

1 Retrieve the file called STAFF.

(This was created in Example 2 of this lesson.)

Here you have a document already containing text that you will now highlight.

To do this, select the text first.

2 Select the heading 'WORD COURSE DELEGATE LIST' (do this either by using the mouse, or by pressing the **<Shift>** key together with the arrow keys).

The heading will now be highlighted.

3 To underline, click on the ⊔ icon or press **<Ctrl>** and U

This text has now been underlined. The highlight will be removed when the cursor is moved from this text.

4 Similarly, embolden the three column headings.

5 Re-save the document as 'COURSE' and close the file.

NOTES

An alternative method of highlighting text is to use the menus. To do this, select the text you wish to highlight and then choose **Format** and **Character** Now you can choose the appropriate style, e.g. Bold, Italic, etc. You are also able to change the type and font size using these commands.

EXAMPLE 6: INSERTING PAGE BREAKS

Insert a page break after the first paragraph in the document WORD2.

METHOD

1 Load WORD2 and display this document on your screen.

2 Move the cursor to the blank line between the first and second paragraphs.

3 Now insert a page break.

Either i) select **Insert** and **Break** and press **<Return>** or click on **OK**

or ii) press **<Ctrl>** and **<Return>** together.

4 A dotted line now appears in your document. This line defines a page break and means that the text starting with the second paragraph will be printed on Page 2.

5 Try using the **File** and **Print Preview** options to show how this document will look when printed.

Pressing **<Page Up>** and **<Page Down>** will enable you to see the other pages previewed.

6 You can delete this page break using the **<Delete>** key if required.

NOTES

The cursor must be at the beginning of the line below the point where the page break is required in order to delete.

7 Experiment with inserting and deleting page breaks within this document.

EXAMPLE 7: INDENTING PARAGRAPHS

Using the WORD2 document, experiment with indenting paragraphs.

METHOD

1 Erase the screen and then retrieve the WORD2 document.

> The WORD2 document contains only a few paragraphs. In this example, we will look at indenting paragraphs. The paragraph you are now reading in this book has already been indented. This means that each line of text within the paragraph automatically begins at a specified tab position. In Word for Windows, the cursor will go back to the left margin only when a **<Return>** is pressed.

2 Now indent the second paragraph in the document.

Move the cursor to the start of the required text.

Either i) click on the ⊞ (indent) icon.

or ii) choose **Format** and **Paragraph**

In the Left indentation box type **1** and **<Return>**

3 This paragraph has now been indented by one inch (or one tab setting) on the left margin.

Experiment with indenting both the left and right margins in this text.

4 Using the **Format** and **Paragraph.** options try a Left Indent of 0.5 and a First Line Indent of -0.5. This will allow you to specify a different position for the first line of a paragraph than the standard indent. This is useful when numbering paragraphs, for instance.

TEST

1 Erase the document on the screen.

2 Create a new document containing the following text. Include underlining , emboldening and centering as shown:

<u>Word for Windows</u>

In this tutorial, we have considered many facilities available in the **WORD FOR WINDOWS** package. Basic functions have been introduced, such as:

1 Creating Documents
2 Saving and Retrieving
3 Inserting and Deleting Text
4 Printing Documents

All the facilities covered here have been accessed using the menus and icons available within **WORD FOR WINDOWS.**

Some more advanced features have also been used, such as those involved in re-formatting documents:

1 Changing Margins
2 Setting Tabs
3 Indenting Paragraphs
4 Changing Print Settings
5 Copying and Moving Text

3 Move the sentence starting 'All the facilities...' down to the bottom of the document.

4 Insert the following text after '4 Printing Documents'.

Although a mouse is preferable, this package can be used without one. Options can be chosen by clicking the mouse button on the required option, or pressing the **<Alt>** key and choosing the option.

5 Indent the last paragraph.

6 Insert a page break before 'Some more advanced features...' and print your document.

7 Save this document and clear the screen.

▬ ▬ ▬ ▬ ▬ ▬ ▬ ▬ ▬ ▬ ▬ ▬ ▬ ▬ ▬ ▬ ▬

FURTHER EXERCISES

1 i) Create a memo layout document as shown below:

<u>ABC COMPANY PLC</u>

<u>COMPUTER SERVICES</u>

From:		**To:**	
Ref:		**Date:**	

_____

SUBJECT:

ii) Ensure that the titles are highlighted as shown, and add tab positions so that a user can move across to input information in the various positions in the memo.

iii) Save this as MEMO1

iv) Erase the screen.

2 i) Retrieve the memo layout created in the previous question (MEMO1).

ii) Input the following details:

From:	J Khan	**To:**	G Smith
Ref:	JK21/6	**Date:**	5/11/93

_____

SUBJECT: SQUASH TOURNAMENT

Following your message dated 1st November 1993, I would like to inform you that the tournament has now been arranged for 4th December 1993. Further details on times and team lists will be available next month.

iii) Save this as file JK21 and clear the screen.

iv) Retrieve MEMO1 and type in a memo from yourself to your Line Manager requesting an increase in pay.

v) Save this as RISE1 and clear the screen.

You are now ready to go on to Lesson 6: Formatting Documents.

Lesson 6:

FORMATTING DOCUMENTS

In this session, we will consider various facilities of particular use when editing large documents.

At the end of this lesson you will be able to:

- number pages
- adjust page breaks
- print out selected pages
- change font types
- use windows.

Load Word for Windows. A blank page will be displayed on your screen.

EXAMPLE 1: INSERTING PAGE NUMBERING

Create a document containing text explaining some Word facilities and print it out with page numbering.

Use the following text in your document:

FURTHER USE OF WORD FOR WINDOWS

1 In the previous lessons in this tutorial we have considered a number of basic facilities available within WORD FOR WINDOWS. More advanced facilities will be introduced in this lesson.

2 Other useful facilities in the creation of long documents include:

2.1 WORD FOR WINDOWS automatically inserts page breaks into a document when it is printed. You are able to change the position of a page break if required.

2.2 WORD FOR WINDOWS will also enable these pages to be automatically numbered when printed.

2.3 WORD FOR WINDOWS will allow you to print out selected pages from the document.

3 Another useful facility is the ability to split the screen into a number of 'Windows' so that you can view different parts of the document, or different documents, at the same time.

4 All of the above facilities will be illustrated in this lesson using this text as a typical example.

METHOD

1 Create a new file and type in the text given above.

(Use the Left Indent and First Line Indent options to help format this document.)

2 Insert page breaks after Section 2 and Section 3. (Use **Insert** and **Break** to insert these at the appropriate points.)

3 Your document is now three pages long. To number these pages:

Choose **Insert**

Choose **Page-Numbers**

4 The Page Numbers window is displayed.

At this stage the position of the page number can be redefined to the top or bottom, and left, centre or right of the page. For this example leave it where it is.

5 Press **<Return>** or click on OK

Page numbers will be placed on all pages other than the first. This is the default setting because often the front page of a document (e.g. the title page) will not require numbering.

NOTES

The page numbers are not displayed, but will appear when the document is printed out.

6 Now print out this document.

Choose File

Select Print

Press **<Return>** or click on OK

The document will now be printed out on three pages with Pages 2 and 3 being numbered.

7 If you wish to number the first page as well you can use an alternative method of page numbering.

Select View

Choose Header/Footer

Now select Footer

Ensure that the Different First Page box does not have a cross in it. Do this by clicking on this box or moving there with the **<Tab>** key and pressing **<Space>**

Now press **<Return>** or click on OK

The first page now contains a page number.

Use File and Print Preview to check this.

If you do not see the full page previewed, try to click on the bottom border and drag it down to make the window larger.

EXAMPLE 2: ADJUSTING PAGE BREAKS

Change the page breaks in the current document and print it out again.

Ensure the document created in Example 1 is displayed on the screen.

METHOD

1 Page breaks can be adjusted in the Print Preview screens as follows:

Choose **File**

Select **Print Preview**

Now choose **Margins**

2 The screen now shows the left, right, top and bottom margins. The page break is also displayed as a dotted line.

Using the mouse, drag this up or down to a new position.

You will automatically see the reformatted pages.

3 Experiment with changing these page breaks. Finally close the Print Preview to return to your document.

EXAMPLE 3: PRINTING SELECTED PAGES

Print out specified pages in your document.

The document currently displayed should contain at least 3 pages. If not, insert extra page breaks using **Insert** and **Break** or pressing **<Ctrl>** and **<Return>**

METHOD

1 To print out selected pages:

Choose **File**

Choose **Print**

2 Move to the **From:** box in the Range section.

Type **2** (Do *not* press <Return>)

Move to the **To:** box

Type **3**

Press **<Return>** or click on **OK**

3 The required range (e.g. pages 2–3) has been printed.

The same print window will also enable you to print only the current page if required.

4 Save this document as a file called FURTHER.

EXAMPLE 4: CHANGING FONTS

Change the type of font used in a document.

METHOD

1 Any document can be used to illustrate this, e.g. the FURTHER document used in the previous examples.

2 Highlight the text you require to change. For example, highlight Section 1 in the FURTHER document.

   Now change the font:

   Select **Format**

   Choose **Character**

3 The Character Window is displayed as shown below:

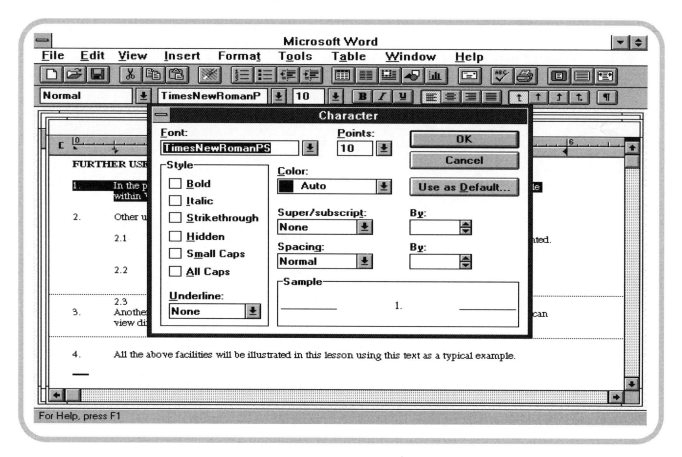

In the Font box press or click on the down arrow.

Other font types are revealed.

Select a different font.

Press **<Return>** or click on **OK**

4 The highlighted section has now been changed to the selected font.

   Experiment with changing the font again using the **Format** and **Character** options. These options will also enable you to change the size of characters using the Points box. Try this now.

5 An alternative method of changing fonts is to use the Ribbon described on page 84.

   Close the document before proceeding.

EXAMPLE 5: USING WINDOWS

Set up Windows in order to display two documents on the screen.

Any two existing documents can be used for this example.

METHOD

1 Open a document, e.g. FURTHER.

Now open a second document, e.g. WORD2.

2 Two documents are now open and can both be displayed on your screen as follows:

Select   **Window**

Choose   **Arrange All**

The following screen is displayed:

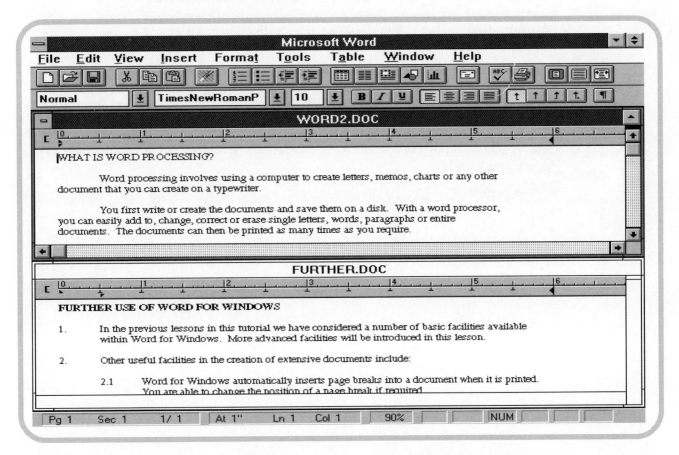

3 The screen is now split into two windows. Only one window is active at any time. The title bar of the active window is highlighted and the cursor is flashing in the document.

You can move from one window to another simply by clicking the mouse at the point where you want the cursor to be, Alternatively choose   **Window**   and select the required file.

4 You can move a window around the screen simply by clicking on the title bar of a window and dragging it to a new position.

5 If you close a document the remaining window will stay in the same position. Close one document now to illustrate this.

Now select   **Window**   and   **Arrange All**   to return to the original full screen display.

6 Close all documents.

TEST

1 Retrieve the WORD2 document.

2 Insert page breaks after each paragraph in this document.

3 Change the font for the second paragraph.

4 Print out this document including page numbers.

5 Split the screen and load the WORD1 document so that you can view both files together.

6 Copy a paragraph from the WORD1 document into the WORD2 document.

7 Exit without saving these changes.

FURTHER EXERCISES

1 i) Load an existing document such as EMPLIST created in Lesson 4, page 40.
   ii) Insert page breaks into this document and print it out with page numbers.
   iii) Change the type and size of fonts for selected text in this document.
   iv) Print out only pages 1 and 3 from this document.

2 i) Load the document EMPLOYEE (created in the Test Section at the end of Lesson 2, page 25).
   ii) This document contains a list of employees together with their grades and salaries. Add extra employees to the list.
   iii) Use the Window facility to split the screen.
   iv) Load a new file (e.g. WORD1) into Window 2.
   v) Copy a paragraph from WORD1 into the other document displayed and re-save the amended document as WORD3.

You are now ready to go on to Lesson 7: Advanced Editing.

Lesson 7:

ADVANCED EDITING

In this session we will deal with many advanced editing features designed to help you use Word more easily and efficiently.

At the end of this lesson you will be able to:

- show non-printing characters
- search and replace text
- check spelling
- set borders
- create tables.

Load Word for Windows. A blank page will be displayed on your screen.

EXAMPLE 1: SHOWING NON-PRINTING CHARACTERS

Load the WORD2 file and show all invisible (non-printing) characters in this document.

METHOD

1 Load the WORD2 file.

2 Show all the non-printing characters.

Select **Tools**

Choose **Options**

The options screen is displayed as shown at the top of the next page.

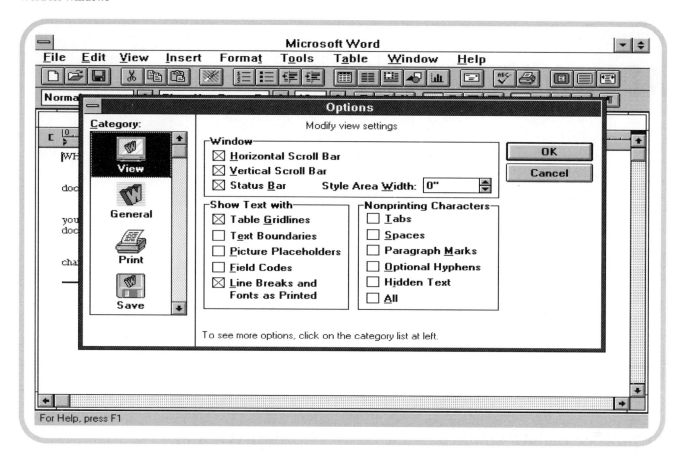

Go to the **Nonprinting Characters** section and change the All box so that an **X** is displayed. (Do this by clicking on the box or pressing **<Tab>** to move to the box and **<Space>** to toggle.)

Now press **<Return>** or click on **OK**

Your document is now displayed including the non-printing characters.

For example, you will see the following characters included in the text:

paragraph marker   ¶
tab character   →
space character   ·

These 'hidden characters' can be used to help edit documents.

3 Try to add and delete tabs, spaces and returns to illustrate how these can be used when editing.

4 Finally select **Tools** and **Options** and return to not showing the non-printing characters by removing the × from the All box.

5 Experiment with other facilities in the Options screen.

NOTES

The display of non-printing characters can also be achieved by clicking on the ¶ icon in the Ribbon (described on page 84).

EXAMPLE 2: USING SEARCH AND REPLACE

Using the document WORD2, find all the occurrences of 'word' in the document and replace with 'text'.

METHOD

1 Move the cursor to the beginning of the document.

2 Choose **Edit** and **Replace**

The following screen is displayed:

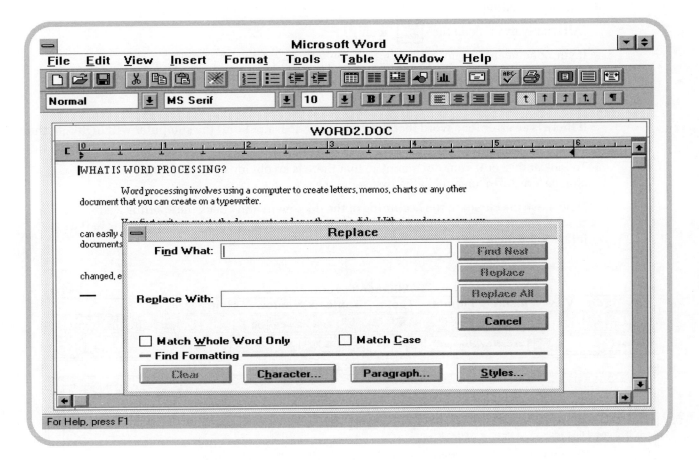

The Replace screen prompts:

Find What?

3 Type in the text you wish to search for:

i.e. **word** (Do *not* press **<Return>**)

4 Use an arrow key or the mouse to move over to **Replace with:**

5 Type in the text you wish to replace this with: i.e. **text**

Now select **Replace All**

Now choose **Close**

6 All occurrences of 'word' have now been replaced by 'text'.

The package deals with upper and lower-case letters (capitals and small letters), so 'WORD' is replaced by 'TEXT' and 'Word' by 'Text', and so on.

7 Change the document back to its original wording by replacing 'text' with 'word'. Remember to move the cursor to the beginning of the document before you do this.

EXAMPLE 3: USING THE SPELL CHECKER

Use the Spell Checker facility to examine the text in your document.

METHOD

1 Display the WORD2 document on your screen.

2 Move the cursor to the beginning of the document.

3 Choose **Tools**

4 Choose **Spelling**

(Alternatively click on the [ABC] icon.)

If your document has no spelling errors you will get a message saying:

The spelling check is complete

If so, click on **OK**

If there is an error (or a word that the dictionary does not hold) the computer will highlight the particular word and suggest alternative spellings.

5 To look at this, edit your document so that there is an obvious mis-spelling. For example, change 'create' to 'creatte' in the first sentence.

6 Now move the cursor to the beginning of the document and check the spelling again. You will see that the mis-spelt word is highlighted and alternative spellings are offered, as in the following screen:

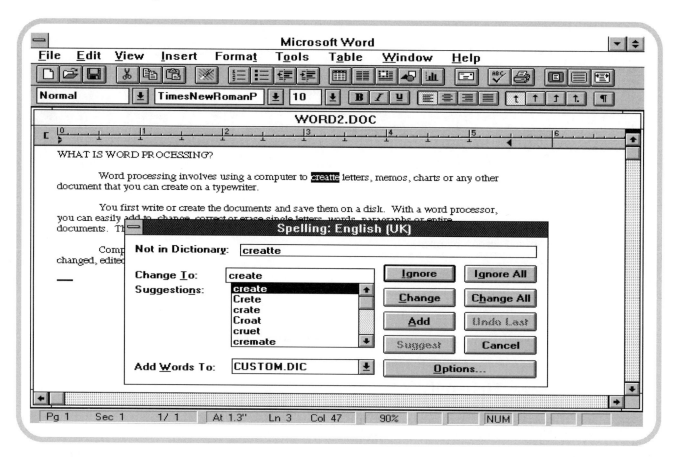

7 Move the highlight to the correctly spelt word (i.e. create) and click on **Change** The mis-spelt word has now been replaced in your document. When words are not included in the dictionary, you can choose the **Add** option.

EXAMPLE 4: ADDING BORDERS

Draw a border around selected text.

METHOD

1 Open a document, e.g.WORD2.

Select the text you wish to draw a border around, e.g. select all the text in the first paragraph. (See Lesson: 4, Example 2 on selecting text)

2 Select **Format**

Choose **Border**

You are now presented with a number of available border lines in the Border Paragraphs box as shown below:

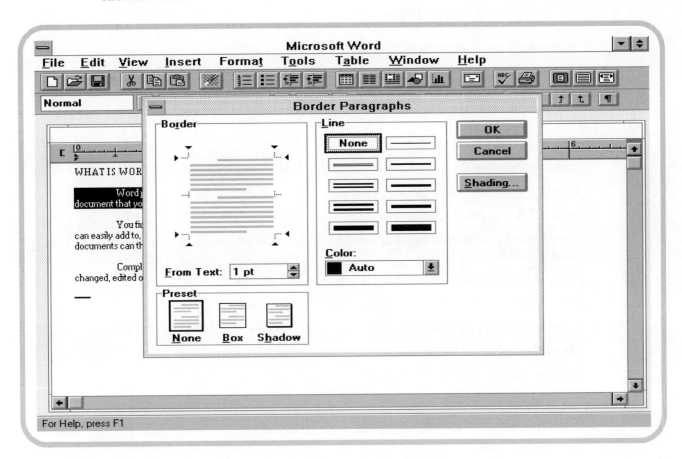

3 Use the mouse or arrow keys to select a suitable border.

Press **<Return>** or click on **OK**

4 The selected text is now enclosed in a border.

5 Borders can be deleted by selecting a Line Type of **None**

6 Experiment with other border types.

You can also shade within the selected borders by choosing the **Shading** option in the Border Paragraph Screen and changing the Custom Pattern.

EXAMPLE 5: CREATING TABLES

Set up and print out a table with borders.

Set up a table containing the following information:

TIMETABLE

Group	9–11	11–1	1–3	3–5
A	Computing	Science	Art	PE
B	Maths	Computing	Science	Art
C	Language	Arts	Maths	Geography

METHOD

1 Open a new document.

Type in the heading **TIMETABLE**

2 Move the cursor to a new line.

Choose **Table**

Select **Insert Table**

Now specify the number of columns as **5** and the number of rows as **4**

Now press **<Return>** or click on **OK**

3 Grid lines are now shown indicating the table. (If not, select **Table** and **Gridlines**)

Type in the details as given in this example.

Press **<Tab>** or use the mouse to move between cells in the table.

If you make a mistake you can edit this text in the usual way using the mouse or arrow keys to move the cursor.

The grid lines shown on this screen will not be printed out.

(You can see this if you choose **File** and **Print Preview**)

4 If you want lines printed around these cells in the table you must define a border.

Select all the cells in the table. These should now be highlighted.

Now choose **Format** and **Border**

Select a suitable line style

Also select the **Preset Grid** display

Now click on **OK**

5 The borders are now displayed around all the cells in this table.

Save the document as TIME.

Print out this table and close the file.

TEST

1 Create a new document called FACIL containing the following text. Ensure that the text is highlighted and that tabs are used where appropriate.

FURTHER FACILITIES IN WORD FOR WINDOWS

This WORD FOR WINDOWS package contains a range of facilities to assist in the production of a document. Such facilities include:

Invisible characters

Spell Checker

Tables

The Spell Checker uses an existing dictionary of words incorporated in the package. New words can be added to this dictionary when necessary.

2 Show all the non-printing characters to check where the tabs and returns are located in the document.

3 Change the tab settings so that the list of facilities is indented more than at present.

4 Change the word 'package' to 'packag' and use the Spell Checker to check the whole page.

5 Draw a border around the list of three facilities listed in the first paragraph, and print the document.

FURTHER EXERCISES

1 i) Create a new document containing the following text:

JOE BLOGGS ENTERPRISES
ESCAPE COMMITTEE

MINUTES OF THE MEETING HELD ON SATURDAY 30 FEBRUARY 1995, AT 4.30 A.M.

Present:	J Godber
	S Riskoff
	T Agadan
	P Pawley
Apologies	J Thomas
	M Munroe

1 MINUTES OF LAST MEETING

Agreed

2 MATTERS ARISING

None

3 ACTION POINTS

It was agreed that J Thomas and M Munroe should escape as quickly as possible.

4 NEXT MEETING

To be held on Sunday 31 February at 3.30 a.m.

ii) Use the Spell Checker to ensure that all the words in this document are correct.

NOTES
The dictionary will not recognise the names, and they will be highlighted as mis-spelt.

iii) Draw a border around the list of those present and those who sent apologies.

iv) Save the document as ESCAPE and clear the screen.

2 i) Retrieve the COURSE file created in Lesson 5, example 5.

ii) Move the cursor to the beginning of the document.

iii) Reveal the non-printing characters to show the tab positions that have been set up.

iv) Now change the tab settings to character positions of 10, 30 and 50. Has the layout of your document changed ?

v) Change the tab settings and margins in this document and preview the result.

You are now ready to go on to Lesson 8: Merging Documents.

Lesson 8:

MERGING DOCUMENTS

In this session we will consider the merging of a document with a data file. This can be useful in many examples, such as the production of standard letters or personalised forms. Note that this is not the same as simply combining two documents together.

At the end of this lesson, you will be able to:

- create a main document
- create a data file
- merge the two documents.

Load Word for Windows. A blank page will be displayed on your screen.

EXAMPLE 1: CREATING A DATA FILE

Produce a list of names and salaries of employees for a data file.

Use these details for the employees:

Jahinger Singh	£19,250
Julia Lewis	£32,520
Louise Jones	£16,500
Margaret Purvis	£18,500
Richard Rees	£25,350
David James	£20,675

A list as shown above can be merged with a standard letter to produce personalised letters.

The list would be referred to as a *data file*.

The standard letter would be called the *main document*.

METHOD

1 For this example we will create a data file, containing the names and salaries given above.

Firstly open a new file using File and New

2 Now select File and Print Merge

The Print Merge screen is displayed as shown at the top of the next page.

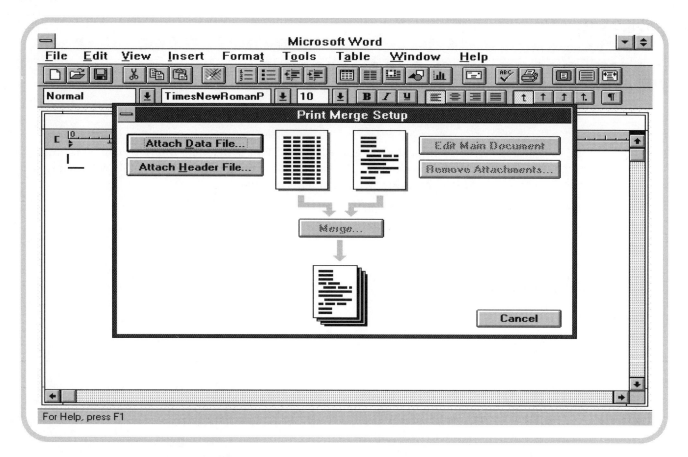

Choose   **Attach Data File**

Now select   **Create Data File**

3   Now you must insert the field names for all the details (i.e. names and salaries) you wish to include in the list. Each detail is contained in a separate 'field' in the data file. In this example you require two fields to be set, i.e. Name and Salary.

In the Field Name Box type   **Name**   and press   **<Return>**   or click on   **Add**

Similarly, type   **Salary**   and press   **<Return>**   or click on   **Add**

You see that **Name** and **Salary** are included in the Fields in Header Record box.

4   Click on   **OK**   to finish.

Now type in a name for the data file.

E.g. type   **NAME1**   and   **<Return>**

The screen is displayed showing a table containing the two fields as shown at the top of the next page.

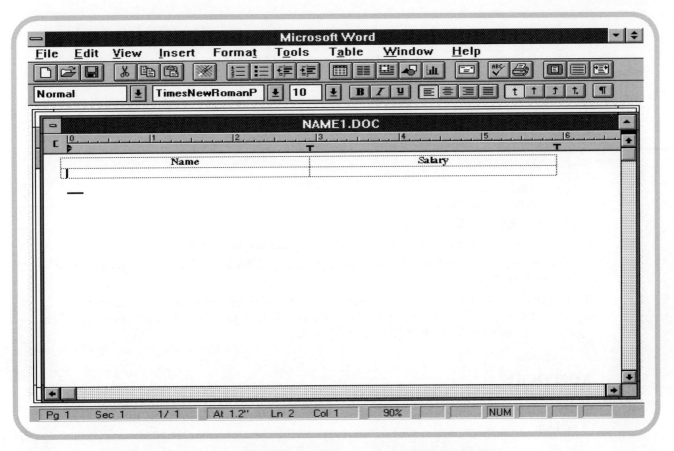

5 Now type the name, e.g. **Jahinger Singh** (Do *not* press **<Return>**)

Press **<Tab>** to move to the next field and type **£19250**

Press **<Tab>** to move to the next row.

A new blank row is created in your table.

Insert the remaining data required in this example.

6 When you have added all the data save this document using **File** and **Save**

7 Choose **File** and **Close** to close this window.

Proceed to the next example.

EXAMPLE 2: CREATING THE MAIN DOCUMENT

Produce a standard memo to employees, containing details of new salaries.

Use the following text in your memo.

<u>**XYZ COMPANY**</u>

To:

From: Alice Zave
            Personnel Manager

SUBJECT: PAY REVIEW

I am pleased to inform you that as from 1 April 1994 your new salary will be

This will be paid in your May salary and backdated to April. If you have any queries please do not hesitate to contact me.

The *main document* is the standard letter, form or memo containing general information. Specific details can then be obtained from the data file (e.g. your list of employees created in Example 1). Here we will create the main document.

METHOD

1 The empty document opened at the beginning of Example 1 should be displayed on your screen.

Now start to type the document:

<u>**XYZ COMPANY**</u>

To:

At this point you need to enter the name of the employee. This name is contained in the data file attached to this document, so here you just need to add in the field.

Select `Insert Merge Field`

Choose an appropriate field, e.g. `Name`

Press **\<Return\>** or click on `OK`

The Name Field has now been inserted and is displayed as **\<\<Name\>\>** in your document.

3 Continue to type:

From: Alice Zave

            Personnel Manager

SUBJECT: PAY REVIEW

I am pleased to inform you that as from 1 April 1994 your new annual salary will be

Now select `Insert Merge Field`

Choose `Salary` and press **\<Return\>** or click on `OK`

The **\<\<Salary\>\>** field has been inserted in your text.

4 Continue typing the remaining text to complete the memo. The completed memo will be displayed as shown at the top of the next page.

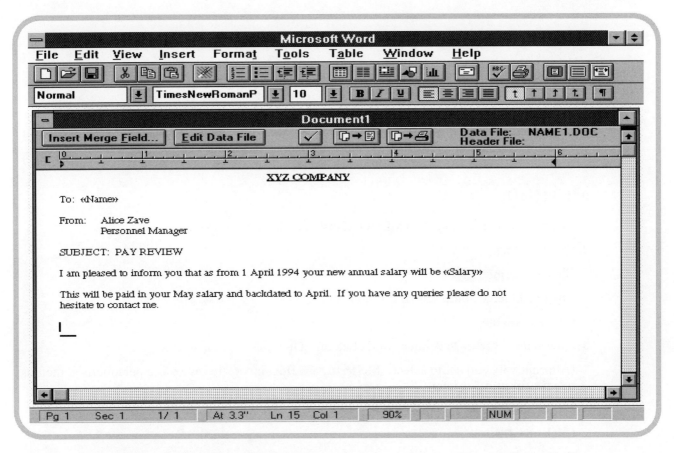

5 Save this document as PAYMEMO.

EXAMPLE 3: MERGING DOCUMENTS

Obtain a print-out of the memo created in Example 2, personalised with the employees' details given in Example 1.

We are going to merge the main document (the memo) with a data file (the list of employees and pay data) to produce standardised memos.

METHOD

1 The main document, i.e. PAYMEMO, should be displayed on your screen.

2 Choose File

Choose **Print Merge**

The Print Merge Setup screen is displayed.

Choose **Merge**

3 Now select **Merge to Printer** and click on **OK**

(Alternatively you could select **Merge to New Document** to save these personalised memos to a file for printing later.)

The Print screen is now displayed.

Click on **OK**

4 The two documents are now merged to produce printed personalised memos.

5 Close the PAYMEMO document.

EXAMPLE 4: PRODUCING A STANDARD LETTER

Prepare personalised letters for four customers using a main document and a data file. Print out the merged documents.

The main document should contain the following information:

Dear

We have received your order for   to the value of   This will be processed as soon as possible.

Yours sincerely

J Kooblin

Sales Manager

Produce copies of this letter for the following orders:

Mr Smith, cucumbers, £45
Ms Jones, letraset, £95.50
Miss Indu, pens, £23
Mr Rahmad, paper, £125

Clear the screen before starting this example.

METHOD

1 First, open up a new document.

Now select **File** and **Print Merge**

Choose **Attach Data File**

Now select **Create Data File**

Type in the field names, e.g. **NAME, ITEM** and **COST** pressing **<Return>** or **OK** after each one.

2 Now click on **OK** to finish.

Give this data file a name, e.g. CUST.

A table is now displayed and you can enter the data given in this example.

Now save this data file and close the file.

3 A blank document is now displayed.

Type the letter given in this Example, inserting appropriate field names using the **Insert Merge Field** option.

4 Save this letter as a file called ORDERS and merge the two documents using the **File** and **Print Merge** options.

The documents have now been merged and the personalised letters will be printed out.

5 Close this file.

TEST

1 Create a data file containing details on the following customers:

Ravi Virdu
1 The Highfields
Borton
063-298-1123

Burt Rinaldi
46 Strange Lanes
Todside
081-892-4242

Stan Toomey
29 The Ridgeway
Brechin
048-29462

2 Produce a letter containing the following:

Dear Customer

We are updating our records and wish to confirm that all details are accurate. Could you please check that the following information on your name, address and telephone number is correct:

Please contact me if the details are incorrect.

Thank you for your assistance.

3 Merge the letter with the list of customers and print out your result.

FURTHER EXERCISES

1 The following letter shows a typical reply from a newspaper to readers' correspondence:

Mr Jarvis
4 The High Street
Chester

Dear Mr Jarvis

Thank you for your recent correspondence regarding the article in our paper dated 2 June.

Your complaint is being dealt with and we will inform you of the outcome in due course.

Yours sincerely

F Payne
Assistant Editor
The Daily Wagon

   i)   Produce a main document containing this letter, leaving space for the reader's name, address and the date specified in the first sentence.

   ii)   Produce a data file containing the following readers' details:

       Mr Jarvis, 4 The High Street, Chester, 2 June
       Ms Smyth, The Grange, Burkenham, 25 July
       Miss Ragu, 26 The Avenue, Brecon, 17 May
       Mrs Rabbitt, 45 Wayside, Ruminster, 12 August

   iii)   Merge these two documents and print out the resulting personalised letters.

2 The following letter could be used during a recruitment procedure:

       29th September 1992

       Mrs M Mansfield
       2 Redwood Avenue
       Chester

Dear Mrs Mansfield

Re: Secretary, Production Services

I am pleased to inform you that following the recent testing session, you have been selected to progress to the next stage in the selection procedure.

I would like to invite you to attend an interview at 2.00 p.m. on Monday 12th October with myself and Mr Lockwood, Production Services Manager.

The interview should last approximately one hour, after which you will have the opportunity to look around the offices.

On arrival, could you please report to the Security Officer who will direct you to the Personnel Department where I will meet you.

If you have any queries please do not hesitate to contact me.

Yours sincerely

Natalie Thomas
Personnel Manager

i) Produce a standard letter, leaving space for the applicant's name, address and the date and time of the interview.

ii) Produce a data file containing the following details on applicants and interview times:

Mr J Bobtail   4.00 p.m. Monday 12th October
22 Dale Road
Winchester

Mrs E Burik   9.00 a.m. Tuesday 13th October
109 Caledonia Drive
Bolton

Ms J Udall   11.00 a.m. Tuesday 13th October
9 Maple Gardens
Caernarfon

iii) Merge these two documents and print out the resulting personalised letters.

This concludes the tutorial on Word for Windows

The final sections in this tutorial include a summary of both the editing features and commands used, and an introduction to further Word for Windows facilities.

ADDITIONAL EXERCISES IN WORD FOR WINDOWS

1 i)   Produce the following menu and ensure that each line is centred and highlighted as shown:

<u>**THE BLUE FIG RESTAURANT**</u>

DINNER

Taramasalata
Prawn Cocktail
Whitebait

* * *

Cream of Mushroom Soup
Consomme

* * *

Roast Beef
Saddle of Lamb
Dover Sole

* * *

Selected Vegetables

* * *

Coffee

   ii)   Insert items of your own choice into this menu.
   iii) Insert selected desserts after the main course, to include Profiteroles and Gateaux.
   iv) Print out the resulting document and save as BLUEFIG

2 i)   Create the following document, giving a list of competitors in a forthcoming gymnastics competition. Insert appropriate tab settings for the required columns.

Time	Competitors	Judges
9.30 a.m.	Andrea Boguti Steve Harris Rick Wyman	R Burnham S Tracey
10.00 a.m.	Ian Strange Sean O'Leary Topu Yan	B Blackley
10.30 a.m.	Lesley Farnham	R Burnham

   ii)   Delete Steve Harris from the 9.30 a.m. session and insert Francis Mackay and Ravi Puri into the 10.30. a.m. session.
   iii) Preview the document, print out two copies and save and close this file as COMP
   iv) Create a new document containing the following information:

11.00 a.m.	Edwin Seir Elsie Allen June Burden	B Blackley

   v)   Combine this document with the COMP file and print it out.

3 i)   You wish to send personalised letters to some of your clients. Produce a standard letter containing the following:

Dear

Thank you for your instructions regarding the property at

We are in the process of preparing promotional material and will advertise this   at a price of

I will inform you as soon as we receive any interest in the property.

Yours sincerely

ii) Place your name at the bottom of this letter and today's date at the top. Save and close this document as AGENT1

iii) Produce a list of clients' details giving the name, address of the property, type and price and shown below:

> Mrs Whittle, 4 Hazel Close, bungalow, £97000
> Mr Burden, 26 Parish Court, house, £175000
> Mr Eaton, 423 Noble Road, flat, £86000
> Miss Gucci, 18 Pine Road, house, £215000

iv) Save this file as VENDOR1

v) Merge these two documents (AGENT1 and VENDOR1) to produce personalised letter to all the clients listed.

vi) Delete Mr Burden and Mr Eaton and insert:

> Mrs Grist, 217 Elm Grove, house, £199000

vii) Print out the personalised letters for the amended list.

4 i) Produce the following document giving the details of a house for sale, using highlighting as shown:

RUMINSTER	**A delightful house in a**
Rural setting	**beautiful woodland area**

DETACHED HOUSE * 3 BEDROOMS * 2 BATHROOMS * LOUNGE/DINING ROOM * SMALL KITCHEN * GAS CENTRAL HEATING * GARDEN SHED AND BARBECUE AREA

<u>Accommodation</u>

Entrance Hall	with stairs to first floor.
Lounge/Dining	L-shaped, 23' x 11' expanding to 16' at one end. Patio doors leading to barbecue area.
Kitchen	Superbly fitted with new Bimbo range of units.

Viewing: Strictly by appointment through the <u>agents</u>.

AGENTS: Gregory & Thomas, Rumble Lane, Ruminster.

ii) Check the spelling in this document.

iii) Insert an extra section under the kitchen details:

Master Bedroom	14' x 9' with ensuite BATHROOM
Other Bedrooms	10' x 11' and 10' x 9'. Both with built-in wardrobes and radiators.

iv) Draw a border around these details

v) Ensure that the layout fits neatly on to an A4 sheet and print out the final document.

5 i) Create the following document, changing tab settings and margins as required, and highlight where shown:

<u>**REDBRIDGE COMPUTER SERVICES**</u>

Tel: 0992-468100

We stock an extensive range of printers and related items. We are sure that you will not be able to obtain such a choice anywhere for the prices quoted.

> **Not only do we guarantee our products for three years, but we also provide all items with an extra print ribbon at no charge.**

The items shown below give some of the more popular products in a range. Contact us for more information.

Item	Code	Price
DIP Printer	D1964	£259.00
RIP Printer	R1965	£299.00
XIP Scanner	X2961	£512.00
TOP Toner	B1007	£25.00 for 10

***If you wish to order any of these items, please call us on 0992-468100 and ask for Bette Davis.

ii) Change the tab settings for the list of items to include an extra column giving information on bulk discounts.

Bulk Discounts

25%
20%
15%
–

iii) Check the spelling in this document and correct where necessary.
iv) Move the block of text beginning 'Not only do we guarantee. . .' to a new position below the items list.
v) Preview this document and print it out.

ALTERNATIVE METHODS

Many of the facilities in Word for Windows can be obtained using the standard keys without using the pull-down menus.

The following summary gives the combination of keys required to obtain the appropriate facilities used in this tutorial.

KEYS	PROCEDURE
F1	Help
F2	Move selected text
F7	Spell checker
F10	Activate menu
F12	Save as
<Alt>	Activate menu
<Alt> F4	Quit Word
<Shift> and arrow keys	Select a block of text
<Shift> F2	Copy selected text
<Shift> F12	Save document
<Ctrl> F12	Open document
<Ctrl> E	Centre text
<Ctrl> F	Change font type
<Ctrl> L	Left align text
<Ctrl> R	Right align text
<Ctrl> S	Change text style
<Ctrl> B	Turn bold on/off
<Ctrl> U	Turn underline on/off
<Ctrl> I	Turn italics on/off
<Ctrl> <Space>	Return to normal text
<Ctrl> ★	Show all non-printing characters
<Ctrl> <Return>	Page break
<Ctrl> <Shift> F12	Print document

FURTHER WORD FOR WINDOWS FACILITIES

This section provides a brief summary of some Word for Windows facilities not included in the preceding lessons. Having completed this course, you should feel confident about exploring additional features contained within the Word for Windows package; the following list will help you to do this.

Any one of the documents that you have already created could be used to enable you to explore these extra options.

OPTION		PROCEDURE
File	Save All	Save all current open documents
File	Summary Info	View or edit summary details on document
Edit	Find	Locate specific text in a document
Edit	Go To	Go to a marked area in document
View	Page Layout	Display document in page layout
View	Draft	Speedy display of document in fixed font
View	Zoom	Enlarge or reduce text image
Insert	Footnote	Insert extra text in document
Insert	Bookmark	Name a location in document
Insert	Annotation	Insert comments on specific sections of text
Format	Style	Use specific pre-set format for selected text
Tools	Hyphenation	Hyphenate words to improve line breaks
Tools	Bullets and Numbering	To improve display of a series of paragraphs
Tools	Record Macro	Start to record a sequence of processes (macro)
Tools	Macro	Run, edit or delete a macro
Help	Help Index	Obtain help and reference information

SUMMARY OF COMMANDS

The following summary illustrates the commands (options) used in this tutorial. The options are obtained from the Word for Windows Menu, by clicking the mouse on the required option or by pressing **<Alt>** and then choosing the option.

LESSON/ EXAMPLE	COMMAND	PROCEDURE
(1.5)	File Save	Saves a document
(1.6)	File Exit	Exits from Word for Windows
(2.1)	File Open	Opens an existing document
(2.4)	File Save As	Saves using a new name
(2.4)	File Close	Closes current document
(2.5)	File New	Creates a new document
(2.6)	Format Paragraph Alignment	Aligns current paragraph
(3.1)	File Print	Prints document
(3.2)	File Print Preview	Preview a document
(3.4)	File Find File	Lists and reviews documents
(4.3)	Edit Cut	Cuts a block of text
(4.3)	Edit Paste	Inserts a block of text
(4.5)	Edit Copy	Copies a block of text
(4.5)	Edit Undo	Cancels previous command
(5.1)	Format Page Setup	Changes page layout
(5.2)	Format Tabs	Changes Tab settings
(5.3)	View	Changes current display
(6.1)	Insert Break	Inserts a page break
(6.1)	Insert Page Numbers	Number pages for printing
(6.1)	View Header/Footer	Edit Headers or Footers
(6.4)	Format Character	Changes font type and size
(6.5)	Window Arrange All	Displays all open documents
(7.1)	Tools Options Nonprinting characters	Turns display of invisible codes on/off
(7.2)	Edit Replace	Replaces one word with another
(7.3)	Tools Spelling	Check spelling in document
(7.4)	Format Border	Draws outline borders
(7.5)	Table Insert Table	Creates a table in document
(8.1)	File Print Merge Attach Data File Create Data File	Sets up a data file for print merging
(8.2)	Insert Merge Field	Adds a field to document if data file has already been attached
(8.3)	File Print Merge Merge	Merges two documents for printing

WORD FOR WINDOWS SCREEN

The illustration below shows some useful parts of the Word for Windows screen:

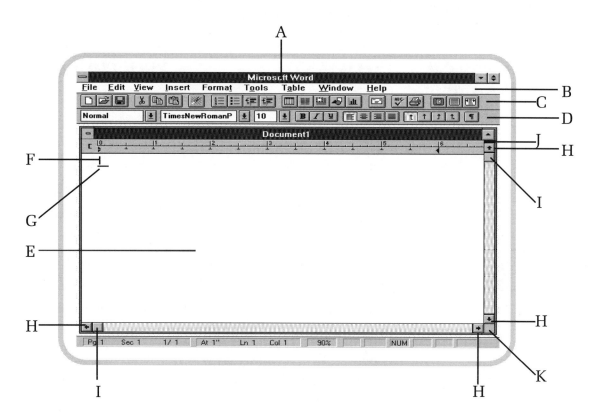

A	Title Bar	Contains the document name.
B	Menu Bar	Used to access required options.
C	Tool Bar	See the following section for details.
D	Ribbon	See the following section for details.
E	Text Area	Type text and graphics in this area.
F	Insertion Point	This shows where the text will be inserted.
G	End Marker	The end of the current document.
H	Arrows	Click on these to scroll around the document.
I	Scroll Boxes	Click and drag on these to move around more quickly.
J	Split Screen	Click and drag down on this to split the screen in two. This will enable you to look at two parts of the document at the same time.
K	Window Corner	Click and drag on this to change the window size.

TOOL BAR

The Tool bar contains a number of icons to simplify many of the commands used in word processing.

The Tool bar can be displayed or hidden by choosing **View** and **Toolbar**

The following icons (or buttons) are available on the standard Tool bar:

	Open a new document.		Insert a table.
	Open an existing document.		Format your document with newspaper style columns.
	Save the current document.		Place a frame around selected text.
	Cut selected text.		Start the Draw program.
	Copy selected text.		Start the Graph program
	Paste text.		Create an envelope.
	Undo the last command.		Check spelling of your document.
	Number selected paragraphs.		Print current document.
	Place bullets in front of selected paragraphs.		Display document in 'page layout' view.
	Remove indent from selected paragraphs.		Display document in normal view.
	Indent selected paragraphs.		Display full width of page.

RIBBON

| Normal | ↓ | TimesNewRomanP | ↓ | 10 | ↓ | **B** | *I* | <u>U</u> | ≡ ≡ ≡ ≡ | t ↑ ↱ ↥ | ¶ |

The Ribbon will enable you to change the appearance of your document very easily.

The Ribbon can be displayed or hidden by choosing **View** and **Ribbon**

The following buttons are available on the Ribbon:

| Normal ↓ | Used to apply text styles.
Click on the arrow to reveal available styles. |

| TimesNewRomanP ↓ | Used to change the text font.
Click on the arrow to reveal other available fonts. |

| 10 ↓ | Used to change the text size.
Click on the arrow to reveal the text sizes available. |

| **B** | Turn bold on or off. |

| *I* | Turn italics on or off. |

| <u>U</u> | Turn underline on or off |

| ≡ | Left justify selected text. |

| ≡ | Centre selected text. |

| ≡ | Right justify selected text. |

| ≡ | Justify (left and right) selected text. |

| t | Set Left Justified Tab. |

| ↑ | Set Centred Tab |

| ↱ | Set Right Justified Tab. |

| ↥ | Set Decimal Tab |

| ¶ | Display or hide non-printing characters. |

GETTING OUT OF DIFFICULTIES

This section contains useful tips on sorting out problems which may occur when learning to use Word for Windows. If you encounter difficulties at any stage in this tutorial, ensure that you have followed the instructions in the text precisely. If in doubt, go back to the beginning of the example. If you still have problems, the following points may be useful.

TYPING TEXT

Remember that there is an automatic 'wrap-around' when inserting text into a document. This means that you can type in text without pressing **<Return>** at the end of each line. The Word for Windows package will do this for you. A **<Return>** is only needed to force the cursor on to a new line, e.g. at the end of a paragraph.

TOOL BAR

This is usually displayed below the menu and contains icons to open and save files, cut and paste text, print documents and much more. (See notes on the Tool Bar in a separate section.)

The Tool Bar display can be turned on or off by choosing **View** and **Tool Bar**

RIBBON

This is usually displayed below the Tool Bar. The Ribbon contains information on the type and size of font used, bold, italic and underline icons as well as alignment and Tab icons. (See notes on the Ribbon in a separate section.)

The Ribbon display can be turned on or off by choosing **View** and **Ribbon**

FILENAMES

When saving a new document, you will be required to enter a new filename. Filenames consist of a number of characters (usually letters and numbers) up to a maximum of eight. No spaces are allowed. For example, filenames such as FILE1, ABC and DOC25 are all acceptable, but FILE 1, AB*C, DOC.25 are not. If in doubt about the location of your documents when saving or retrieving, specify the drive as well as the filename, e.g. A:FILE1, C:DOC25, etc. (see *Saving and Retrieving* below).

SAVING AND RETRIEVING

Your computer is set up to save and retrieve files from a given directory or drive, e.g. Drive A or Drive C. When you **Save** or **Open** you can select the appropriate drives and directories containing the documents. When opening files a filename can be typed in or selected using the mouse from the list displayed.

SELECTING OPTIONS

When selecting options from the menus provided in Word for Windows a variety of methods can be used. Firstly, a choice can be made by using the mouse to click on the required option. Alternatively, press **<Alt>** to activate the menu, then either:
i) move the highlight on to the required option using the arrow keys and press **<Return>** to choose the option, or

ii) type the single underlined letter of the required option.

MENUS

The main Word for Windows menus can be activated while you are editing a document by pressing the <Alt> key or using the mouse. An alternative way of obtaining many of the editing facilities is to use the Tool Bar and Ribbon located below the menu. If these are not shown select the View option to turn the display on.

MOVING THE CURSOR

To move quickly around the document you should use the mouse in the scroll bar situated to the right and bottom of the screen.

The arrow keys on the key board can be used to move the cursor around a document. To move around more quickly use the <Ctrl> key together with an arrow key. Other keys such as <Page Up> and <Page Down> can also speed up moving around your document.

PRINTING

If you have problems obtaining a print-out of your document, check that the printer is connected and set up correctly. You may need to do this using the Print Manager available in Windows. When Word for Windows is first installed, the printers to be used must be specified. You can change a printer specification by selecting File and Print Setup from the menu. You can then change the printer settings (such as printer type) as required. At this stage, if you press <F1> you will obtain a list relating to the highlighted option

HIGHLIGHTING

It is quicker to highlight (e.g. underline, embolden) while you are entering text than afterwards. Do this by using the icons on the Ribbon. Alternatively, using the keyboard, the <Ctrl> key together with U (for underline), B (for bold), or I (for italics). Normal text can be obtained by pressing <Ctrl> and <Space> The alternative is using the Format and Character options to go back and highlight text already entered.

TABS

When you insert a Tab in a document, an invisible (nonprinting) character is inserted into the text. Choose Tools and Options from the menu to show all non-printing symbols symbols. Using this facility you will be able to see where all the tabs are. This may help you when editing your document.

LISTING FILES

If you cannot remember the name or contents of a file you wish to edit, use the File and Find File options to obtain a list of files. Filenames will then be listed on the screen and you can move the highlight to the filename required in order to display the contents of the document.

SHOWING INVISIBLE CODES

This is a useful technique to assist you in editing your document. Use Tools and Options to display all the nonprinting symbols. Characters such as tabs, paragraph markers, spaces and new line markers can all be displayed if required.

MERGING DOCUMENTS

Note that this is not the same as combining documents. 'Merging Documents' refers to merging a main document (e.g. a standard letter) with a data file (e.g. a mailing list) to produce personalised documents.

The two files can be linked by attaching the data file to the main document using the **File** and **Print Merge** options.